LISA G. FISCHBECK

Foreword by Samuel Wells

BEHOLD

WHAT YOU ARE

Becoming the Body of Christ

T0161764

CHURCH
PUBLISHING
INCORPORATED

Church Publishing
19 East 34th Street
New York, NY 10016
www.churchpublishing.org

Cover design by Gillian Whiting
Typeset by Denise Hoff

A record of this book is available from the Library of Congress.

ISBN: 978-1-64065-323-8 (paperback)
ISBN: 978-1-64065-324-5 (ebook)

Contents

Dedicated to the People of The Advocate

Foreword

This is a book of wisdom. The conventional way to be wise is to disappear to a secluded place, away from other human beings, sit in your cell, and let your cell teach you everything. Lisa Fischbeck hasn't done that. She has faithfully ministered to one congregation for many years—and has let that congregation, and most of all the church's liturgy as lived by that congregation, teach her everything. She has chosen the better way.

It is the definitive claim of the ethics of virtue that the actions in which you have become habituated are revealed most explicitly at a moment of crisis; as Iris Murdoch puts it, "Decisions are what we take when we've tried everything else." When the unexpected happens, disaster strikes, usual procedure is impossible—then the world sees what you're really made of. More than once in this book Lisa Fischbeck recalls moments when something has "gone wrong" during a worship service: most commonly, a congregant is taken seriously ill. Such a moment is like a cross-section of a tree: it reveals what a community and its leader are really about. If everyone panics, tries to suppress the truth, pretends it isn't happening, then you know, painfully and undeniably, that what's happening is a performance, and, like viewers at home watching a live broadcast, the show must go on in such a way that no one notices. But if this really is the Body of Christ, and if the suffering of the hand affects the flourishing of the foot, the leader is more likely to say, "You may have noticed that one of our number has been taken ill. I'm glad to say emergency support is on its way. But of course we're all anxious for her. I'm going to say a brief prayer to place her in God's loving embrace, and then we'll resume our worship." Not only does such action deepen the ligaments of Christ's Body, it models to all present how to locate every setback and shock of their lives within the larger pattern of devotion and faithfulness. Such is the wisdom expressed in this book.

This is a book of renewal. Out of anxiety, many congregations and their leaders seek a technique to get evangelism right, a template to make worship more attractive, a sales pitch to draw strangers to events or gatherings. But renewal is based fundamentally on trust. This book is testimony to the extraordinary things that happen when you trust the Holy Spirit to show up. Ministry is about creating the right environments where the Holy Spirit can reliably be expected to show up. Lisa Fischbeck displays those moments, those environments, and that trust. The definitive such environment is the Eucharist. Every action of the worship service is precisely such a moment when the Holy Spirit can reliably be expected to show up. My theology professor at seminary asked me a telling question about my congregation a few months after I was ordained: "Is there an atmosphere of expectation before the service?" Thirty years on, I've never heard a better way of discovering whether or not a congregation was in good shape. By probing worship on high days and holy days, Lisa Fischbeck digs deeper and deeper into the soil from which renewal comes. Sit in your worshiping congregation, and your worshiping congregation will teach you everything.

This is, finally, a book of prayer. Prayer is the moment our full humanity meets God's full divinity. Jesus is the definitive embodied prayer, because he is fully human and fully divine. Again, the conventional way to pray is to go into a quiet room, close the door, close your eyes, and wish for something to happen. This is a much more incarnate vision of prayer than that. Here the ordinary meeting and greeting, preparing and tidying, handshaking and hugging all become part of what we mean by prayer. Like in Montessori schooling, our attention is quickly directed to the precious quality of the materiality of our lives. We hold things in two hands, trusting that if we do simple things well, greater things will be revealed through them.

Together, wisdom, renewal, and prayer constitute the fruits of forty-two years of the author's experience of the Episcopal Church, and decades of ministry within it. Lisa Fischbeck's book crystallizes that experience and makes it available to God's church. She has done a beautiful thing. She has described how humanity comes face-to-face with God.

Samuel Wells
January 2021

Preface

In the chapel of the monastery of the Society of Saint John the Evangelist, at the conclusion of the eucharistic prayer, the presider raises the consecrated bread and wine and declares to the people, "Behold what you are." The congregation replies, "May we become what we receive." The exchange, derived from the writings of St. Augustine some sixteen hundred years ago, reminds those who have gathered that through their participation in that liturgy, they will become the Body of Christ that they already are. More and more.

Liturgy expresses what we believe and forms what we become. It is a public and communal act, open to all. It often happens in a church around the Eucharist on Sunday but can significantly happen on other occasions and in secular spaces as well. Increasingly, it happens online. In the church's liturgy, whenever and wherever it happens, we are called together by God to be and to become the Body of Christ—the church.

Behold What You Are is written to open up the possibilities of liturgy and liturgical awareness, in the church and of the church, Sunday by Sunday, lifetime by lifetime. Writing started long before the Covid pandemic, but the dramatic shift to online worship occurred as the deadline for the manuscript loomed. Surprisingly, the concepts and practices encouraged for in-person worship readily translate to worship online. With thoughtful reflection and intentionality, the public expression and formation of the Body of Christ in liturgy can be more vital for all.

This book is the result of forty-two years of life formed by the liturgy of the Episcopal and Anglican Church. I write as a woman who was initially drawn to the Episcopal Church on the campus of Southern Methodist University in Dallas, Texas. The St. Alban's chapel at the Canterbury House there was beautiful and simple, intimate, and informal. My questions and my doubts were welcomed, and the liturgy brought the faith to life for me and allowed me to claim that I could be a Christian. As I moved from Texas to Virginia to North Carolina, I experienced the worship, fellowship, and organization of the Episcopal Church more broadly. I explored the church on other continents and dug deeply into the roots of the church in England. The liturgy nourished, sustained, and excited me season by season, year by year.

This book is especially born of the last eighteen years of my life as a missionary priest, a "planter" of a twenty-first-century expression of Episcopal Anglican tradition at the Episcopal Church of the Advocate in Chapel Hill, North Carolina. Launched in 2003 with the support of three established parishes and a bishop who encouraged us to be rooted in the traditions of the church but not bound by them, The Advocate emerged as a faith community with a lively, engaging, and participatory liturgy.

This book tells the story of that emergence, and also the foundation on which it was built. Parts of *Behold What You Are* will read as a refresher for some and news to others. Sections will be confusing to some readers and exciting to others. The book is presented with a desire for Episcopalians and those of the liturgical sacramental tradition to robustly engage in the planning and practice of the liturgy. My intention is that readers will grow more and more aware of the power of that liturgy to express and form the people of God as the Body of Christ, given for the world, loving God and one another with forgiveness, sincerity, and joy.

Acknowledgments

My appreciation goes out to the Most Rev. Michael Curry who cheered me on and went to bat for me when the going got tough in the early days of The Advocate; Charis Bhagianathan at Episcopal Church Foundation Vital Practices, who helped me to claim an identity as a writer; Joe Rose of the Trinity Retreat Center in West Cornwall, Connecticut, who provided a space to write; and Nathan Kirkpatrick, who stepped up at The Advocate so I could take time away. I am grateful to Mary Ogus, the patient and honest alpha reader; to Joslyn Schaefer and Sadie Koppelberger for content recommendations; to Diane Stoy, the scrub editor, and Alice Graham Grant, who offered edits to the final draft. Most of all, thanks to my daughter, Rebecca Bland, who embraced The Advocate as her sibling, and to my husband, Lamar Bland, who has provided steady support and presence all along the way.

1 | Liturgy as Public Expression and Formation of the Body of Christ

When I was a child, my father worked in the research labs of the Radio Corporation of America (RCA). It was the 1960s. My father relished his part in the technological revolution that was changing our society and our world. Innovations in communications—lasers, televisions, printers—were all part of his daily life and dreams. His excitement was contagious.

On our road trip vacations, my father encouraged us to search for the RCA logo wherever we went, and he led us in singing John Philip Sousa's "Stars and Stripes" any time we passed an RCA building or store. My father's strategy kept us alert and engaged along the way. When we passed through a developed area, I kept my eyes searching for that logo. When I spotted one I shouted, and the car burst into song.

That simple family tradition planted the seeds of my appreciation for ritual and liturgy, and it influenced my life as a priest. Yearning, expression, formation, and belonging were all there. The practice enfolded me in my family—this is something that we do. The ritual also gave me a sense of being part of something larger than my family or even the town where I grew up. RCA was everywhere.

Through familiar and beloved rituals, with or without our knowing, human beings express what we believe and are formed by what we do. As a college student in the 1970s, I experienced the unexpected victory of my school's football team in an intense rivalry. The fans stormed onto the field, crowding around the winning goal post, climbing, pulling, and tugging until the goal post came loose. They lifted it up and passed it around the crowd, with arms stretching to touch it or to help move it along. The goal post moved through the fans and was carried around the stadium, then out into the main campus. After parading the goal post through the quadrangle, the exuberant fans deposited it on the steps of the university chapel and cheered. Every person who witnessed the procession of the goal post that day felt the joy of victory. All who touched the goal post tangibly participated in that joy.

Consciously or not, in ways large and small, our actions express and form our values and priorities—what we believe about ourselves, our communities, our world, and our place in it. Our credit card statements, social media activity, emails, reading and shopping habits all reveal our beliefs. Weight loss programs, sports teams, and political campaigns help us express and form our identities in the secular world. Summer camps for children include rituals such as singing camp songs and setting candle boats out into a lake. Colleges and universities offer orientation programs for incoming freshmen to promote community through the intimacy of small group experiential education. Life in the military builds upon a sense of community as a matter of life and death.

Citizens are familiar with the rituals of government. Each year, the president of the United States delivers the State of the Union address. Every branch of government is present. The Supreme Court justices wear their black robes, elected members of Congress sit according to their political affiliation, and the vice president and the Speaker of the House sit near the president. Each year, at the appointed hour, the sergeant at arms of the House of Representatives announces the arrival of the president, and the president walks in to applause and cheers, shaking hands left and right while moving closer to the podium. Some of this protocol is written, some is tradition. The event is scripted. Whether we agree with the president's address or not, the ritual and liturgy of the annual event remind us of who we are as Americans and how our government is structured. The State of the Union address helps to shape and form us as American citizens who witness and participate in it.

Every day, communities gather at secular cathedrals large and small—soccer fields, racetracks, sports arenas, the gym, shopping malls, the office—where common values are reinforced through shared rituals and practices. On Sunday mornings at the local food cooperative, food and drink are fresh and healthy, and the open and expansive seating area is crowded with local residents who come to eat well, see their friends, visit with like-minded people, and listen to live music.

Ten miles from the Church of the Advocate in Chapel Hill, North Carolina, a twenty-first-century shopping mall looms as a secular cathedral,[1] with vast space, commercial iconography, ritual foods, and rhetoric that beckon and form the worshipper. The success of shopping malls and their online equivalents depends on a baseline understanding of anthropology and psychology, as well as sophisticated marketing research that reveals trends and desires. Savvy secular marketers form faith and shape believers.

Parades, rallies, marches, annual festivals, and celebrations also form community. For example, at the annual "Procession of the Species" in Olympia, Washington, thousands of residents come together to celebrate and learn about native and threatened animal species. The residents create costumes and musical instruments for a parade described as "a ritualistic celebration of the natural environment, building solidarity, responsibility, and community, . . . a personal yet public experience."[2]

From labor marches to gay pride parades, from royal enthronements to waves in football stadiums, human beings realize the power of collective movement. Cave drawings, ancient mosaics, and tapestries all reveal the importance of processions and parades in the lives of our ancestors. Parades were woven into the social fabric of American life, with saint's day parades in ethnic Roman Catholic neighborhoods and rodeo and circus parades on the western frontier. For years, ticker tape parades in New York have welcomed and feted soldiers, astronauts, and soccer stars, providing a means for those gathered along the route to express their joy, admiration, and pride. And every four years in Washington, DC, inauguration parades celebrate the nation and a new presidential term. At the 2017 Women's March in Washington, DC, pink hats and chants unified and energized a collective of creative individual expressions. As the hours passed and the numbers exceeded all expectations, those gathered realized that they were not alone. The sea of pink hats was a force to be reckoned with.

These examples reflect the human impulse to create expressive actions, rituals, customs, and traditions, and our openness to be formed by them. This book is born of a passion for greater awareness, intentionality, and thoughtful creativity in the church's rituals and liturgies, that worship may become even more expressive and formative for the people of God.

Questions for Reflection

1. Can you think of a particular public/secular event or practice that has been meaningful to you?
2. What faith or belief does that "liturgy" express?
3. How does it form the belief and identity of those who participate in it?

Church Liturgy: As We Pray, So We Believe

As early as the fifth century, the Church proclaimed *lex orandi, lex credendi*. The law of praying is the law of believing, or as more commonly stated, "As we pray, so we believe." What Christians believe is expressed by what we do and say in worship. What we say and do in worship forms what we believe and what we become.

Members of the Episcopal Church have a love of the liturgy, or at least an appreciation of it. The sacraments, particular movements and postures, and the theological nuance of the prayers carry great meaning for those who have been formed by decades of weekly practice. The familiar and resonant words of the canticles, and the Prayer of Humble Access from Rite I still echo in their souls: "But Thou art the same Lord whose property is always to have mercy. . . ."

However, there are many in our churches who have not yet found meaning in the liturgy's rhythms. They recognize the pattern of songs, the readings, the Peace, and the Eucharist. They see the clergy enter the church at the beginning of the service and leave at the end. They may sense the arc of the liturgical year, though some in the congregation only know Pentecost as "the day we wear red." Without regular attendance week in and week out, even faithful members may miss the education and formation that evolves as the seasons move from the anticipation of Advent to the outpouring of the Holy Spirit on Pentecost.

Visitors and newcomers to an Episcopal church may have grown up in a liturgical sacramental setting but may not have thought about it since they were confirmed or married. They may have no church background at all, may think the liturgy is intriguing, but are not ready to participate in an adult confirmation class. How we present and enact our rituals, then, is a crucial matter of hospitality.

Individuals gain some formation simply by being present for the church's worship, yes. But there is so much more to be gleaned, expressed, and understood in order to experience a more vital liturgical experience. Since ritual and liturgy express and form the faith of those who participate in it, those who plan and execute the liturgy have an obligation to consider carefully both spoken and written words of hospitality and explanation.

Ritual and Liturgy

A vital step toward hospitality and meaningful participation in liturgical practice is understanding the distinction between ritual and liturgy. Rituals depend on familiarity with the actions that are performed over and over again, often in the same place, and even in the same pew. Rituals may be private or public, individual or collective, done alone or in a group. When the world around us seems unsteady or chaotic, we turn to ritual as an anchor.

At its best, ritual connects us with time-transcending truths and comforts us. Ritual shared with others connects those who share it into a certain unity of being. Ritual elements of our liturgy include the *Sanctus*—Holy, Holy, Holy—and the words of institution—"On the night he was betrayed he took bread, said the blessing, broke the bread, and gave it to his friends, and said, 'Take, eat: This is my body, which is given for you. Do this for the remembrance of me. . . .'" These are words spoken by Christians who have gathered since the beginnings of the church some two thousand years ago. The lifting of the elements at the conclusion of the prayer is an iconic image that even those who have never been in a church would recognize as ancient and sacred.

I propose that liturgy, however, is always a public work, and is always done by a congregation of people. Liturgy does not depend on familiarity, although it is certainly enhanced by understanding. Liturgy can be designed uniquely for a particular place and occasion. Liturgy often includes ritual and is grounded by it. Ritual within the liturgy provides a stability and consistency that we yearn for and need. Liturgical acts or words often become ritual over time. The aptly named "comfortable words" now found in Rite I of the 1979 Book of Common Prayer (BCP, 332) are a prime example. Generations of Episcopalians could recite them: "Hear the Word of God to all who truly turn to him. Come unto me, all ye that travail and are heavy laden, and I will refresh you" (Matthew 11:28). The words became ritual because they speak a truth we all long to hear: Jesus publicly invites and welcomes us and our burdens.

Words and actions, predetermined and consistent from Sunday to Sunday, season to season, year to year, can become a bedrock, a reliable routine. In a world that is changing at an accelerated rate, many religious people find comfort in knowing that when they begin the liturgy on any given Sunday morning, they know what to expect. This is why any change in our liturgy is often met with conflict and adversity. Change can be a fearful thing.

Ritual transcends time and location and is the same whenever and wherever it is practiced. Liturgy contextualizes the ritual and varies through time and place. The liturgy in Advent is similar yet different from the liturgy in Eastertide. The liturgy in a cinder-block chapel in Haiti is similar yet different from the liturgy in a grand cathedral in midtown Manhattan. Liturgy is an expression of the people gathered, and the people gathered will be formed by the liturgy—the oft-repeated rituals, as well as the prayers, music, and movement of a particular occasion and location in which they come together.

In settings grand or simple, a liturgy can be life-giving, soaring, or soothing. It can express the beauty of holiness and heal the wounded soul. Regardless of the setting, a liturgy can also be hollow, dry, disconnected, and painfully exclusive, especially to the uninitiated. A liturgy may reflect the mystery of God, but it need not be mysterious itself. This is why we need to regularly reexamine the works, words, and actions of our liturgy.

It is said that in the original Greek, liturgy was a public work done on behalf of the people. It had a certain connotation of *noblesse oblige*, the rich providing for the needs of the public. Today, the idea lives on in the concept of a public works department, providing water and other services for the common good. In the first millennium of the church, the word was adopted with an understanding that the service and worship of the church was also for the public good. The liturgy came to mean all the worship services of the church, and more pointedly, the Mass, the eucharistic rite. The liturgy was understood as the movement, ritual, and words of that rite. With the liturgical renewal movement in the second half of the twentieth century, liturgy was defined as "the work of the people." It was the work of the congregation, as well as a public work. The current online glossary of the Episcopal Church defines liturgy as "the church's public worship of God." It "expresses the church's identity and mission, including the church's calling to invite others and to serve with concern for the needs of the world."[3]

In my own teaching and practice of liturgy, I have incorporated elements of all of these meanings, defining liturgy as a public work, performed by the people gathered, through which we express what we believe and are formed in what we become. If liturgy is a public work, then the public should know that it is happening and that it is happening for them. This means among other things, that liturgy is about hospitality, and that those who perform the liturgy remain ever mindful of the "strangers" who might be present. If liturgy is the work of the people, then liturgy is best crafted in a way that engages the people gathered as fully as possible. If liturgy expresses what we believe and forms what we become, then those who craft the liturgy and many who participate in it are able to articulate what each action expresses about our faith and how it forms us in our faith.

Scripted reminders, either aloud or in print, give welcoming formation to the visitor and the curious, describe why we are about to do what we are about to do, and encourage the formation of the regular participants. Subtle changes in the Sunday liturgy can alert us to the meaning behind the ritual, revealing things that have been understood previously only by the initiated or the trained, and engaging those gathered in being and becoming the Body of Christ.

Becoming the Body of Christ

Christian liturgy is an expression of Christian faith given to us in scripture and tradition—creation, fall, promise, and hope. It is the story of the beauty, wonder, and mystery of God, of who we are as creatures of God, and of how we are at once unworthy *and* worthy to stand before God. It is also the story of the church as the Body of

Christ, given for the world. This was the metaphor given by Paul the Apostle in his letters to the church in Corinth, Ephesus, and Rome:

> For as in one body we have many members, and not all the members have the same function, so we, who are many, are one body in Christ, and individually we are members one of another. (Romans 12:4–5)

> The cup of blessing that we bless, is it not a sharing in the blood of Christ? The bread that we break, is it not a sharing in the body of Christ? Because there is one bread, we who are many are one body, for we all partake of the one bread. (1 Corinthians 10:16–17)

> But speaking the truth in love, we must grow up in every way into him who is the head, into Christ, from whom the whole body, joined and knitted together by every ligament with which it is equipped, as each part is working properly, promotes the body's growth in building itself up in love. (Ephesians 4:15–16)

In our eucharistic rite, when we pray for the Holy Spirit to come and transform the bread and wine of the Eucharist (the *epiclesis*), we pray that it would transform us as well: "Unite us to your Son in his sacrifice" (BCP, 369).

And, in Eucharistic Prayer 2 of *Enriching Our Worship* (62) we pray: Pour out your Spirit upon these gifts that they may be the Body and blood of Christ. Breathe your Spirit over the whole earth and make us your new creation, the Body of Christ given for the world you have made.

Then we recall the words of Jesus as he blessed and broke the bread and gave it to his disciples saying, "This is my body, take and eat this in remembrance of me."

This "remembrance," from the Greek *anamnesis*, is more than recounting a fond memory. It is, rather, bringing the physical, the person, back among us by re-membering him. We take and eat the bread, in communion with Christ and with one another, and Christ is re-membered in and through us.

The collects and prayers affirm this belief as well. On the Feast of All Saints, we pray to God: You have knit together your elect in one communion and fellowship in the mystical body of your Son Christ our Lord (BCP, 245).

We are the Body of Christ. It is in our scripture and our rites. Ours is a corporate, a communal faith—from God in three persons, to God who becomes one with us all by becoming one of us all, to our being sent forth into the world as one body.

This belief that our individual selves are part of a larger body, and that our identity as part of a body gives meaning to our life and work in the world, is at the heart of Christian faith and tradition. It is also in keeping with the human desire for identity and belonging that is so often expressed in our secular liturgies. Even so, this corporate and communal faith and identity runs counter to the culture of much of what has evolved as "American Christianity" with its emphasis on individual salvation.

From our beginnings as a nation, the United States has valued rugged individualism. Although the church was a center for social gathering and formation, Christian faith developed as a personal matter, not to be discussed publicly. It often emphasized the importance of individual conversion and a personal relationship with Jesus.

The liturgical renewal movement of the latter half of the twentieth century served as a corrective to privatized faith and life, at least in liturgical sacramental churches. With it came a shift and a renewed focus on the congregation gathered and on the Eucharist. Altars were moved away from walls so that presiders could stand facing the people. Chairs started to replace pews, which allowed for greater flexibility of space and movement. Private baptisms were discouraged. The rites of the Episcopal Church were changed, ultimately becoming the 1979 Book of Common Prayer.

Congregations moved from saying "I believe" to "We believe" when reciting the Nicene Creed, providing a more accurate translation of the Greek and recognizing that the creed articulates the faith of the church, not only the faith of an individual within it. The exchange of the Peace was reintroduced from centuries of dormancy and extended through the congregation. The Prayers of the People became more truly the prayers *of the people* and were led by deacons or lay readers rather than by the presider. These prayers allowed for a call and response from the congregation and encouraged intercessions and petitions. Most significantly, the Eucharist, with its offering, blessing, breaking, and partaking, became the central act of worship on Sundays and feast days.

Since the late twentieth century, society and culture have become even more individualized and privatized. Television and the internet have increased awareness of the wider world and promoted more global ways of thinking, but also have led to increased polarization and separateness. Neighbors often do not know one another, and earbuds and live streaming isolate us even further.

Church at its best provides an alternative narrative to the privatizing, divisive trends of our time. Church is a place where we can be together, sing together, and eat together. Church is a place where we gather to celebrate and mourn, to make sense of the world around us, and to share our confusions. Church is a place where we experience those who can comfort us and also challenge us in love. Church is a place where unity can overcome estrangement, forgiveness heal guilt, and joy conquer despair (BCP, 429). At its best, the church's liturgy emboldens us to carry that experience of unity, forgiveness, and joy with us into the world.

Church is a place where, ideally, we persevere in engaging with one another when estrangement, guilt, and despair threaten to isolate us from each other. The call to love one another encourages that perseverance, as does the baptismal covenant: "Will you seek and serve Christ in all persons, loving your neighbor as yourself?"

Church is a place where we learn about and experience those who are beyond ourselves and our kin, and where we are called to engage with them, whether or not they are members of our own community of faith. Church is a place where we learn about God, the "loving, liberating and life-giving God"[4] revealed in scripture, in sacrament, and in the actions of the faithful.

Church is a place where we discover and claim our identity as the Body of Christ. Words and prayers, movements and moments, all born of intention, remind us that we are one with Christ and one with one another, in the world and for the world. Thus, when we are sent forth from the church as the Body of Christ, we go forth knowing that we are part of something greater than our individual selves and our individual households.

Unlike secular communities and organizations, the church is not only a body of people with a shared purpose and mission. We are not just any body, we are Christ's Body. We go forth knowing that we are not alone. We have one another and we have the assurance that nothing will "separate us from the love of God" (Romans 8:38–39). As the Body of Christ, we are called to join with others as a reconciling presence that helps to restore the people of this world to one another and to the God who created them.

We are the Body of Christ, given for the world. This means that, just as Jesus was present to the poor, the outcast, and the marginalized, so are we. Just as Jesus spoke the truth to power, so do we. Just as Jesus walked the way of God's love and God's peace in a world torn by injustice and violence, we walk that way as well.

Borne by our faith expressed and formed in liturgy, we know we are cared for, cared about, forgiven and loved, even as we care for, care about, forgive and love others, sometimes at great sacrifice. With God's forgiveness and hope in our hearts we go forth, whether from a church building or from a computer screen in our living room. We go forth, not for our own aggrandizement or promotion, but we go forth as one body, to heal the torn fabric of our world, in the name and the way of Christ.

Being Open to the Serendipitous

Ritual anchors the liturgy and also anchors the formation of the people in the practice of the faith. At the same time, liturgy can become more vibrant and the formation of the people enkindled when those who preside are open to the peripheral and the spontaneous. The anniversary of an event in our common life, a call to prayer emerging from our national life, a revival of an ancient custom, or the creation of something new provide opportunities for exceptional liturgical action.

Opportunities for spontaneity occur in the routine Sunday liturgy as well. Sometimes, the most expressive and formational moments in liturgy happen when we break from the ritual, or when we place it in a new and unexpected setting. Surprising and unexpected liturgical moments can form us as individuals and as community most profoundly. Often, a single spontaneous event within the liturgy expresses and forms the faith of those gathered more than an entire season of the predictable and reliable. The unexpected teaches us something about ourselves, about others in our community, and about God that we might not otherwise realize.

We experience this when the power goes out just before the liturgy is to begin, when we decide to worship outside because it's a beautiful day, when a child spontaneously starts singing "We'll Walk in the Light" in the middle of our prayers, or when the priest sets aside her sermon and speaks unscripted from the heart; when a visitor arrives in a wheelchair, and the order of procession must change to accommodate him; when a train rumbles by in the middle of the eucharistic prayer and the celebrant pauses, allowing the congregation to relish the moment; when we hear a helicopter heading to a nearby hospital, and we pause for a silent or spoken prayer for the unknown patient on board.

Decades ago, I was worshipping in the Chapel of the Cross in Chapel Hill, North Carolina, when, in the middle of the liturgy, an elder collapsed in her pew. Emergency responders were called and determined that she needed to be taken to the hospital. As she was carried out of the nave on a stretcher, the rector led us in a recitation of the *Nunc Dimittus*:

> Lord, lettest now thy servant depart in peace,
> according to thy word.
> for these eyes of mine have seen the savior. . . .

I was young and impressionable. That moment with the spontaneous deviation from the liturgy gave me a profound instruction of how life and death are framed in the church's narrative. The experience increased my awareness of myself as part of something that transcended time, space, history, and experience—the Body of Christ.

Twenty years later, I met with people from the Christ Episcopal Church in Bay St. Louis, Mississippi, as part of Mission on the Bay, a response to the devastation of Hurricane Katrina on the Mississippi gulf coast in 2005. We worshipped in an inflatable Quonset hut structure that looked like a giant marshmallow. We heard story after story of worship experienced in the weeks after the hurricane swept through, and when the people gathered on the cement slabs where their church used to stand. In shock, in grief, in hope and thanksgiving, the people were united, formed as the Body as never before.

In 2016, at the Church of the Advocate, Kathryn was diagnosed with amyotrophic lateral sclerosis (ALS), also known as Lou Gehrig's disease. By the spring of 2018, Kathryn could no longer walk or talk, restricted to a motorized wheelchair and speaking through a speech-generating device on her computer. Kathryn was keen for others to know and understand ALS. She was also aware that those who were new to the congregation did not know her before she was stricken by this debilitating disease. She asked if she could have a few minutes in the context of the announcements to tell the congregation what her life was like after living with the disease for two years. Instead, we included Kathryn's remarks in the sermon, framed on either end by the vicar's response to the readings and prayers of the day, which included the collect, in which we prayed that we would be "devoted to God with our whole heart, and united to one another with pure affection."

The congregation listened carefully to every electronically produced syllable, as Kathryn began: "I would like to thank you all for your prayers for my health and my husband and caregiver Joe. . . . You have not seen much of us because it takes two to three hours for me to shower and dress each day."

Kathryn's words in the context of the sermon became a liturgical moment. Her words expressed the faith of the people gathered: The Body of Christ, who we are, includes the broken and unexpected. The Body of Christ, who we become, welcomes, knows, and embraces the broken and the unexpected. Members of the Body of Christ care for one another with pure affection. When one part of the body suffers, we all suffer.

Our shared experience of Kathryn's outward and visible brokenness formed us to better embrace the brokenness of others, as well as our own. It also made a world of difference to Kathryn, as she was able to claim her voice and realize herself as a part of the body in a profound and faith-building way. The people gathered were formed by that shared experience, formed as the Body of Christ.

Question for Reflection

1. When have you experienced a moment in church when it felt like a break from the scripted was called for? What happened?

Deviations from ritual can be deeply formative, especially when surrounded and anchored by familiar ritual acts. When we can experience the life-giving possibilities of the movement of the Spirit in liturgy, we are formed to be more alert to the life-giving possibilities of the Spirit throughout the rest of our lives.

Expressive and formational liturgy has a lot to do with ritual—the repetition, the communion with others, the movement, the words, and the songs. It also includes the context and the particulars of time and place, making known the Spirit of God, enlivening and creative, ever moving within us and among us all. The greater our attention to and our intention about our rituals and our liturgical expressions, the more prepared we are to uphold the unpredictable opportunities for grace within those expressions, and the more effective and vital our liturgy may be in forming us to be the Body of Christ, alive and on the move.

When my daughter was a child, I taught her the *Phos Hilaron* (O Gracious Light):

O Gracious Light, pure brightness of the everliving
    Father in Heaven,
O Jesus Christ, holy and blessed!
Now as we come to the setting of the sun, and our eyes
    behold the vesper light,
we sing you praises O God, Father, Son and Holy Spirit,
You are worthy at all times to be praised by happy
    voices. . . . (BCP, 118)

We recited or chanted it together many nights at bedtime, or evenings when the sun hovered on the horizon. It is only as I write this chapter that I realize the parallel of this practice with the singing of the "Stars and Stripes" on the car rides of my childhood. Yearning, expression, formation, and belonging were all there. Perhaps the ritual connected my daughter with her family—this is something that we do. Perhaps it also gave her a sense of being part of something larger than her family or even than the church in which she was growing up. God is everywhere.

Questions for Reflection

1. Can you describe an experience of a church liturgy that formed your identity as a member of the Body of Christ?

2. Can you describe an experience of being a member of the Body of Christ in the world?

2 | Formed by the Sunday Eucharistic Liturgy

It is not uncommon for Michael Curry, the presiding bishop of the Episcopal Church, to inject into a liturgy or sermon, "Turn to the person next to you and say, 'I'm glad to be here and I'm glad you're here too.'" This is similar to exchanging the Peace, although the "I" makes this a personal claim that evokes an uneasiness for many in the pews or chairs who may feel a bit awkward or embarrassed. However, if we go along, we can push past the discomfort and find ourselves more invested in the liturgy, and more vividly aware of ourselves and others nearby.

Many come to church to nurture their faith and to grow in their individual, personal relationship with God in Christ. Much liturgical planning is based on providing a worshipful experience for those in attendance, to help participants know that this old world and the worries of life are not all there is, and that God is there for them. As one person told me early in my ministry, "I come to church to get a handle I can hold onto through the week."

Whether we are aware of it or not, whether we are intentional about it or not, our liturgy and our liturgical space express and form not only our individual relationship with God, but also our relationship with the Body of Christ. Worship, like ritual, can be done individually and alone. Liturgy, the expression and formation of the Body of Christ, takes place in the company of others. Through liturgy, we are transformed from individuals gathered to a people gathered. Our individual selves do not disappear, but are folded into the communal being. The simple act of greeting one another and saying, "I'm glad you're here" can catalyze this awareness and this transformation.

The Advocate is a church without an organ. When we gather for worship, online or in person, we hear the "people's prelude," which is the sound of people greeting one another, conversing, and laughing. This collective voice represents the balance between our identities as individuals and our identity as a people gathered. Each of us brings a unique experience of the world and a unique expression of the holy into our midst. We bring our concerns, our needs, our gifts, our blessings. We meet one another, we speak, we listen, we take things in, and we are reminded that God is in this place, among us. We are here to be and to become a body together. One participant observes,

> I never recognize that we are in the midst of the people's prelude until it is called to a close by the vicar welcoming us and saying "we have had the people's prelude and will now have a period of silence to prepare for worship." In that period of silence, I often wonder at how the people gathering and greeting each other makes us ready to meet God in that moment. As all the wide range of emotions that accompany social interactions melt into readiness and openness, we remember that we are the church because we gather to worship.

Eastern Orthodox theologian Alexander Schmemann wrote of this transformation from individual selves to a people gathered:

> The journey begins when Christian people leave their homes and beds. They leave, indeed, their life in this present and concrete world, and whether they have to drive fifteen miles or walk a few blocks, a sacramental act is already taking place, an act which is the very condition of everything else that is to happen.
>
> For they are now on their way to constitute the church—to be transformed into the church of God. They have been individuals, some white, some black, some poor, some rich, they have been the "natural" world and

a natural community. And now they have been called to come together in one place, to bring their lives, their very "world" with them and to be more than what they were: a new community and a new life.[5]

In every place of worship, from the moment we arrive, what we see and experience enhances or inhibits this transformation. Are we greeted or not? Are we welcomed? Is there any guide for seating or for what comes next? If so, what is in writing and what is spoken? What is assumed? Are we met with silence, the sounds of conversations, or the sounds of an organ? Each sends a particular message about what is important to those who plan the liturgy, and about what we can expect. Over time, such customs and practices help to form the faith and identity of those who worship in a particular place.

The furnishings and the architecture function the same way. Enter a worship space and what do we see? Are there kneelers? Chairs or pews? Facing forward or facing each other? Is there a stage? A flag? A screen?

Churches with round or square architecture evoke the experience of God in our midst and invite the community to draw together. They were likely designed specifically to foster a sense of the immanence of God, as shown by a Quaker meetinghouse with benches that face each other. Over time, worshipping in a circle or facing each other, those gathered begin to believe more fully that God is within and among them, and that the Body of Christ is those who worship together.

On the other hand, churches that draw us up and away, with vaulted ceilings, pews facing forward, and a cross suspended high overhead—the huge Gothic cathedrals and their imitators—evoke faith in God who is transcendent, out there, up there, and away from there. The Body of Christ is more likely to be understood as time-transcending and triumphant.

Of course, God is both immanent and transcendent. Liturgy, at its best, helps us to realize both the immanence and the transcendence of God—God is with us and beyond us, too. God created and still creates the universe and all that is in it. God became a human being to know us intimately by moving within us and among us all. The transcendent God calls us beyond ourselves and the troubles of this life. Christ the King enthroned on high in heavenly splendor, choirs of angels and archangels, are among the images that emphasize God's transcendence. Our hearts swell and our spirits soar. In contrast, it is in the still small voice, in the tender care of another in our time of need, in a reconciling exchange of the Peace, that the immanent God is made manifest.

Good liturgical space and movement will strike a balance between our identity of ourselves as individuals with our own needs, passions, interests, and faith, and our identity as a part of the people of God, the Body of Christ. Similarly, who we are as the Body of Christ is shaped by a liturgy that balances our awareness of the immanence and the transcendence of God. Liturgy that leans into the immanence of God helps us realize that the Body of Christ is our particular congregation and our community. Liturgy that leans into the transcendence of God can help us realize our place in a more transcendent, cosmic Body of Christ. Good liturgical space and movement, even online, will help us to know and experience both realities.

The people's prelude at The Advocate ends when the bell tolls. The bell is a Tibetan singing bowl. The rich, deep, lingering tone calls to us from beyond ourselves. The sound is our first clue that we are here to worship a God who is not just among us, but beyond us too.

Liturgical Welcome

The rubrics for the beginning of the Holy Eucharist Rite II in the Book of Common Prayer are delightfully simple: *A hymn, psalm, or anthem may be sung.* No word about candles on the altar, no word about welcome, no word about procession. How the rubrics are augmented in practice and by words to help the worshiper know what to expect and what to do varies across the Church. In some churches, there is a spoken welcome and instruction, while in others, written guidance is provided.

Some will argue that too many instructions or announcements at the start of the liturgy will overload the listeners, who will not remember them. Others argue that after the liturgy has begun, verbal instructions should not be given because the flow will be interrupted. Many agree that instructions and guidance belong in the printed bulletins. But bulletins are expensive and labor intensive to provide. Bulletins also presume a literate congregation and are not always suited for a particular worship setting. A verbal welcome and instruction create more of a God-among-us feeling, which some will appreciate, and others will find inappropriately chatty or folksy.

Nonetheless, a scripted welcome, with the same carefully crafted words and phrases, offered aloud or in print Sunday after Sunday, serves both to invite the visitor and remind the regular attendee: "This is what we are about." Explaining the setting and the next steps is a significant expression of Christian hospitality.

Welcome to the Advocate.

Here we take seriously the ancient word for worship: the Liturgy. It means the work of the people or the public work. It expresses what we believe and forms what we become—the Body of Christ.

God has brought us together in this place on this day to engage in that public work. Every one of us here will make this liturgy what it is today. It would be different if you weren't here.

So we ask that you participate as fully as possible. When you sing, sing loudly. God loves to hear God's people sing. When you pray, pray boldly, ideally so that we can hear and join our prayers to yours. And if you are called to be still, we ask that you do so mindful of the Spirit of God, moving in and among the people who are gathered here with you.

We will now have a period of silence in which to prepare ourselves in heart and in mind to worship God together in this place. That silence will begin with a bell to call us into it, and when the bell tolls again we will stand and sing as guided by our cantor.

Thoughtfully augmenting the rubrics can make the liturgy more comprehensible and welcoming for all. This augmentation then becomes an integral part of the formation of the people who gather. At The Advocate, the welcome concludes with an invitation to a period of silence, in which we prepare ourselves in heart and mind to worship God together. That word "together" is important here. Each of us is worshipping God, but importantly, in *this* gathering in *this* chapel, or on *this* screen, at *this* time, we are very much worshipping God *together*. Beyond our time together we can make time and space for individual worship as each finds meaningful.

At The Advocate, we sit facing each other. It's hard to ignore each other when we face each other. After a while, we may actually connect facing each other with what we believe about God and about faith. The way we are distracted by each other can be holy. We are meant to be aware of each other. Being mindful of the other, bumping up against the other, with a small "o," can serve to make us mindful of the Holy One, with a capital "O," in whose image we all were created, and also that we are one body, even though we have many different parts. It is good to take the time in silence to prepare ourselves, individually, in heart and mind, to worship God together, as the people of God.

Questions for Reflection

1. Have a look at the rubrics for the eucharistic liturgy in the Book of Common Prayer. Can you identify ways in which your own Sunday worship augments these simple instructions with local tradition or practice? What is gained by that augmentation?

2. Can you identify ways your local practice could be augmented even more, or less, to better express and form the congregation as the Body of Christ?

Processions

On July 4, 1976, I attended liturgy in celebration of our nation's bicentennial at the National Cathedral in Washington, DC. After the music for the opening procession began, I turned to see who and what was coming up the aisle, and saw people bowing for the cross as it passed them. It was like a wave at a football game with heads going down, heads going up. A nominal Presbyterian at the time, with no experience of such embodied reverence, I was amazed. What a powerful visual experience of faith and humility. In that moment, I was invited to be a part of it. And I was given something to do. I could bow!

As noted in the first chapter, human beings by nature realize and celebrate the power of collective movement. Throughout history and across the world today, at sporting events and civic celebrations, on high holy days and saints days, and at weddings and funerals, people dance and move together in processions as lively as ever.

However, at the beginning of the Reformation, parades and processions in England and Northern Europe grew increasingly dignified and stately. In Protestant and Anglican churches throughout Europe and the United States, exuberant processions became the constrained steps of clergy and worship leaders, with the congregation looking on.

An opportunity lost.

The liturgical renewal of the late twentieth century revived the procession of the baptismal party to the font or other source of water and baptism by immersion. Processing the gospel book into the midst of the congregation and reading it there was encouraged. Otherwise, little changed in the practice of processions. In cathedral settings, processions on high holy days or regular Sunday services can be spectacular, with long aisles, powerful choirs, bold organs, the swelling singing of hymns, and crosses lifted high that allow us literally and metaphorically to powerfully express and form faith in an almighty and awe-inspiring God.

Translation of these movements and moments in many churches weakens when the procession serves only to move the clergy and choir into and out of their places, or to signal the start and end of worship, and not much more. The gospel processed only to and from the chancel steps misses a moment for engagement and formation. Holy days, such as Palm Sunday, may involve a perambulation around the outside of the church, but too often lose the opportunity to express and form the faith of clergy and congregation alike.

With greater awareness, a little creativity, and an exploration of the practices of other faiths and corners of Christendom, processions (especially in small and medium-sized churches) can become remarkably formative, expressive, and even evangelical events in the life of the people. Those who process often find meaning in the ritual of the procession. The procession can become more meaningful to the congregation when all participants are included physically, visually, or audibly.

We begin with the entrance rite.

I lived for a while in the country, where a blue-tailed skink lived beneath the railroad ties that marked my small yard. When I mowed, I had to move the railroad ties to fully cut the grass. One summer evening, I lifted a tie, only to see the skink in a nest with a cluster of eggs. Her instinct was immediately to encircle the eggs with her body and tail. Around that circle she moved, gently touching each egg with her nose, as if making sure it was there, tending to it, embracing each as best a mama skink could do.

The image of the skink encircling her eggs is reminiscent of Jesus's lament over Jerusalem in Matthew and Luke: "Jerusalem, Jerusalem, the city that kills the prophets and stones those who are sent to it! How often have I desired to gather your children together as a hen gathers her brood under her wings, and you were not willing!" It's an image that inspires a kind of procession that encircles the congregation rather than splits it down the middle.

Many congregations of the Episcopal Church begin the liturgy on the first Sunday in Lent with the Great Litany, which is chanted in the context of the opening procession. It is customary in many of those churches for the procession on that day to process as a figure eight, moving down the center aisle, then back up a side aisle, down the center aisle again, back up the other side aisle, then down the center aisle one last time, and up into the chancel where the clergy, acolytes, and choir take their places as the litany comes to its conclusion. I wonder why we reserve this procession for the Great Litany on the first Sunday in Lent?

When we process in a figure eight, which also is an infinity symbol, we make known God's encircling of God's people gathered. Cross, gospel book, and presider move around and among us, calling us together for prayer and sacrament, and forming us as a people who are cared for and tended by God.

The meeting hall for the annual convention of the Episcopal Diocese of North Carolina is vast with delegations from more than one hundred twenty-five congregations that require seating for more than five hundred. Although effort is made each year to rotate delegations through the front and center seats, some attendees inevitably feel as if they are in the hinterlands, far from the dais and the action.

This is especially true for the Eucharist, which is held in the convention hall at the beginning of the gathering. As diocesan officials and the bishops process straight down the middle of the wide rectangular space, those to the far right or the far left might only see the top of the processional cross or the tip of the bishop's miter.

Two years ago, a change was made to a figure eight procession, and every congregation was invited to have a representative carry their church banner in the procession. This increased participation and connection for everyone. Now the procession draws the whole gathered assembly in its wake as it moves in a figure eight throughout the large room. Those who chose can make eye contact with those who pass by. Those on the outer edges feel included and liturgically embraced.

"Ah," you may be thinking, "but in our church the side aisles are too narrow for such a procession. People will bump into each other, they won't be able to keep singing when the procession goes by." This too can become a formational moment. Those who must adjust to the procession are reminded that Christ coming among us can indeed be an inconvenience. We may have to adjust our customary stance or practice to make way.

The gospel procession can be formative as well. In recent decades, the gospel is carried, often accompanied by acolytes and song, from the altar to the midst of the people, where it is then read or chanted. These gospel processions have helped to influence the congregation's experience of the gospel reading's centrality to our worship. The congregation is engaged in the gospel by way of a call and response at the beginning and the end of the reading: "The Gospel of the Lord." "Praise be to you, Lord Christ."

What if we borrowed a practice from Jewish worship with the procession of the Torah? For those gathered in the synagogue on a Saturday evening, there comes a time in the liturgy when the Torah scroll is removed from the Ark and processed by the rabbi throughout the congregation. As it passes by, congregants know it represents the Living Word, and reach out to touch it with their hand, prayer book, or prayer shawl. This ritual engages the congregation in the procession and helps them to revere and anticipate the words written in the scroll. Christian liturgy could similarly affect the people gathered if it included in the procession of the gospel book an invitation to bow or to touch the book as it goes by.

> **Cantor:** As the gospel passes by, you are invited to reach out with a touch, a kiss, or a bow, in response to the good news you have heard.

One woman in the congregation noted, "When the gospel is processed in a figure eight after being read, I always have the kind of uncomfortable moment that invites me to grow. Will I reach out? Will I kiss my fingers first? How has hearing the gospel today moved me to act? How is this passage resting it in my body? It is a brief and good uncomfortable feeling that invites a moment of personal reflection on the gospel before switching gears to the homily."

The Offertory

The offertory procession provides another opportunity for the congregation to engage and to move.

Because the bishop of Haiti cannot visit St. Innocent's Church and School in Ticotelette on La Gonave Island very frequently, members of the congregation may wait for years to be confirmed. Only those who have been confirmed by the bishop are allowed to receive communion. Because of this, the not-yet-confirmed tend to leave for home after the offertory, and the offertory procession becomes the high point of the liturgy for them, a crescendo.

Not one, but a half dozen different choirs present their best to God. A children's choir, with some children younger than five years old, includes a solo by a girl no more than ten. The teenaged boys are next, smiling and nodding to the choir of teenaged girls that will follow. The adult choir keeps it going with more than one song in their repertoire. While the choirs sing, the people come forward, dancing, sliding, clapping, and singing along. A girl and her mother carry a basket of eggs. Another household brings tomatoes. A small boy carries a live chicken and ties it to the leg of the chair that has been placed in front of the altar. Some put coins in a plate. And everyone moves their bodies, claps their hands, smiles, and laughs for more than half an hour.

What a contrast this is to the representational offering so familiar to mainline Protestantism and the Episcopal Church. The rubrics in the Book of Common Prayer (361) read:

> Representatives of the congregation bring the people's offerings of bread and wine, and money or other gifts, to the deacon or celebrant. The people stand while the offerings are presented and placed on the altar.

Once again, the congregation, in the role of observers rather than participants, witnesses the collection of each one's money as part of the collection going forward. Formative, yes. But how could the formation be made more robust if the "representatives of the congregation" were *the whole congregation*? What if, instead of sitting and passing a plate, the people came forward with their offerings, as is the practice of churches in Haiti, parts of Africa, and many Baptist churches in the United States? What if, in addition to money and checks, the people of the church brought food for the hungry and food for the fellowship meal that follows the service? Imagine the people coming forward, young and old, hearty and infirm, each offering themselves, as well as gifts from the many resources they have been given, to share with the church or with God's people in need.

The "offertory sentence" is that part of the rite when the celebrant invites the people to prepare for the Eucharist by giving something of themselves to God. The Book of Common Prayer (376) provides several options, taken from scripture, such as:

Ascribe to the Lord the honor due his Name; bring offerings, and come into his courts. (Psalm 96:8)

Walk in love, as Christ loved us, and gave himself for us, an offering and sacrifice to God. (Ephesians 5:2)

These sentences are declared by the presider, at the end of announcements, if announcements have been inserted there, and before the offertory song, hymn, or anthem is sung. But there is so much more that could be said or offered in print. Carefully repeating the same words Sunday by Sunday so they become internalized, the presider or the printed service guide could say:

The liturgy continues with the offertory procession. I invite you to come forward from the waters of baptism (pointing to the baptismal bowl or pool) to the altar, remembering that the most important thing you can give to God is yourself, your soul, your body, your mind. You can symbolize this offering with a simple nod or a solemn bow as you approach the altar. And as you have gifts from the many resources God has given you, to share with the church or with God's people in need, I invite you to leave those at the altar as you pass by. Our offertory includes a hymn . . .

This is lengthy, for sure. But it is an introduction to a stewardship of self and of resources that encourages the people to move and to put their bodies into worship.

Connecting the offering with the offertory hymn or anthem clarifies that as well as ourselves and our resources, we give our voices to God. A choir, if there is one, offers their voices on our behalf. From the beginning, The Advocate's offertory has included food for the local Interfaith Council food pantry. This is not to serve as an end to our contributions to the wider community, but rather as an expressive and formative symbol. If we give a bag of beans in the liturgy, we will be formed in the practice of giving to the world.

A man carries a canvas bag full of groceries for the local food pantry, while a child carries a single can. A parent stops at the baptismal bowl to teach his daughter how to dip her fingers in the water and cross herself, saying "Remember that you are baptized." Some toss rumpled dollar bills into the basket, while others carefully place a neatly folded check.

One after another, the people bow. Self-conscious, some offer just a quick kind of sideways nod as they brush past the altar. Others stop and take a deep and solemn, bend-at-the waist kind of bow. A nonagenarian moves slowly, as does a man long crippled by a stroke. Their bows seem somehow even more reverential, showing a respect for the God who has been with them through it all, and garnering the respect of those who bear witness. A diaper-wearing toddler does a deep knee bend squat, rising to stand again with an alacrity that astonishes anyone over age fifty, and turns to look for his mother.

This offering of ourselves, our souls and our bodies, as well as our resources, takes time that is not as much as the offertory in Haiti, but more than a four-verse hymn or choir anthem. It is time well spent, though. For this time is used to teach and to help the people of God to become and to be the people of God. At the offertory we present our gifts, our very selves to God, offering all to be received, blessed, and transformed.

Bring the offerings of your lives and come into God's courts.

The Prayers of the People

The liturgy provides an opportunity for us, individually and collectively, to express our desires and petitions, our yearning, and our hope. Every Anglican liturgy includes prayers of intercession, and in the Book of Common Prayer, these are called the Prayers of the People. The Prayers of the People are the prayers particular to those who have gathered, and they are also prayers that are universal to the entire Body of Christ, the Church. When we pray as that body, we are, especially in that moment, one with the One who sits at God's right hand, intimately whispering in God's ear.

The 1979 Book of Common Prayer significantly expanded the choices for the Prayers of the People and who could lead them. Six forms are provided, as well as a list of categories for inclusion in prayers (383):

> The Universal Church, its members, and its mission
> The Nation and all in authority
> The welfare of the world
> The concerns of the local community
> Those who suffer and those in any trouble
> The departed (with commemoration of a saint when
> appropriate)

In the Church of England, the prayers are often written and offered by a layperson. These prayers include the different categories and weave in themes of the week's lectionary texts, as well as current events in the world and local community. Varying the prayers from week to week keeps the congregation alert, provides for the expression of the needs and desires of those gathered, and further forms them as the body, the body that prays together for one another and the world. Moreover, the opportunity to write the prayers and to work with the priest or deacon is formative for those who craft them. Episcopal congregations may also use this opportunity to fashion their prayers as a community.

Every form of the Prayers of the People includes space for offering intercessions specific to the people in the congregation. Every form of the Prayers also provides for the people to offer their own intercessions in silence, although the time for personal prayers is often brief, and even rushed, barely giving enough time for the one who prays to think of a single name or situation. If the liturgy is to form us as a people of prayer, providing enough time for a person to articulate a prayer, in heart and mind, if not in voice, is essential. Thus, the period of silence.

In small and even medium-sized congregations and in more intimate settings, the people can be encouraged to share their intercessions aloud. The congregation is then able to hear and to share the concerns that others express. In addition to transitory situations and circumstances, individuals become known for their particular passions, and the community learns what prayers others hold as a spiritual discipline. One man bids prayers each week for the clergy and people of the Diocese of Jerusalem, a woman prays for restorative justice in our criminal justice system, while another prays for peace and justice in Haiti and Zimbabwe and someone else prays for the homeless and the unemployed. Beautifully, on a Sunday when a particular member of the congregation is absent, another member offers up prayer on their behalf, perhaps not with the same words, but with the intent of the one who is absent that Sunday. All these prayers are expressions of the Body of Christ. An intern reflected on this experience of the Prayers of the People: "When I offer a prayer I have an almost physical sensation of that prayer being held up by the collective intention of the gathered body. Hearing the voice of the people during the prayers of the people reminds me of both our diversity and our unity."

Importantly, the presider can further guide the people's formation and identification as the Body of Christ given for the world by offering intercessions "for the people of this congregation in all their varied vocations and ministries in the world." When appropriate, specificity can enhance this formation and identification. For example, one week the presider could add, "especially for those who use their gifts in healing ministries" or "those who use their gifts in teaching."

Instructions and guidance can be given in print or said aloud: "Intercessions are encouraged. Please pray loudly, so we are better able to join our prayers to yours." Or, "After each bidding, I invite you to share your prayers with the whole congregation, so that we may join our prayers to yours. Before we pray together, let us, in silence, ask the Spirit to bring to our consciousness those things for which we should pray." When pauses are plentiful, intercessions are more likely to flow freely.

There are times when the prayers offered are a little too opinionated. Someone could pray that legislators would vote a certain way on a particular bill, or that God would chasten those with opposing opinions. When this happens, the congregation squirms with discomfort.

We may not always like what others pray. But God does not put limits on our prayers and neither should we judge the prayers of others. At the same time, the Prayers of the People are not only the prayers of the individual, they are the prayers of the people, as Sam Wells reminds us, "making the church a community of character and witness rather than making the individual fit for heaven."[6] We offer our prayers mindful of the gathered community. This isn't the time for self-indulgent engagement with God at length and in detail about all the things that anger or hurt us, nor the things that particularly send our spirits soaring. It is a time to pray as the people of God. It is a time to be further shaped as the Body of Christ. As a practice, we might begin to consider before we offer a prayer aloud, "How does the prayer I want to offer help to express and form the people gathered as the Body of Christ?"

Thanksgivings differ from intercessions. Intercessory prayers are offered on behalf of another, placing their needs before God and/or inviting God's presence, healing, and peace in their lives. In prayers of thanksgiving, we give thanks to God on our own behalf, or on behalf of our community, not asking God for anything.

Traditionally, the church teaches that all things for which we give thanks are enfolded in the Great Thanksgiving of the eucharistic prayer. And certainly, all that we are and all that we have are included under "the innumerable benefits procured unto us" (BCP, 335), and in the death, resurrection, and ascension of Jesus.

But specificity matters to the human heart. Following a hurricane, a congregation may need to give thanks for the new day. Those who have worked for more than a decade to build a new worship space will give thanks for the building in which they now gather. The squirm of a child and a baby's cry invoke thanksgiving for the infants and toddlers among us, for their presence as our own and Christ's members. The joy expressed by one can be cause for thanksgiving of the whole. Intercessions for the one being treated for cancer may, in a later season, be followed by thanksgivings for that person's remission.

Humility, kindness, and sensitivity are appropriate to thanksgiving. One person's healing may cause another still suffering to wonder why healing has not come for them. One person's childbirth is difficult for another who has had a series of miscarriages and is now realizing that she may never be able to bear a child. One person's joy for a house being spared in the hurricane is matched by the sorrow of another person left bereft by a total destruction of their home. If

Prayers of the People are to be offered aloud, and are to be prayers of the people gathered, guidance and thoughtfulness are needed. One possibility is to combine thanksgiving with intercession at every turn. Even as we give thanks, we pray for understanding, faith, and an awareness of God's presence "in the midst things we cannot understand" (BCP, 481).

The Eucharistic Liturgy

The Eucharist is the heart of the Sunday liturgy, when bread and wine are offered and taken, blessed, broken, given and received. We hear the story of creation, of God's self-revelation, and of the salvation of the world given in Jesus Christ. We are reminded of what it means to be Christian. We sing, we move, we give ourselves and our lives to God. We witness the change of the bread and the wine, the "fruit of the vine and work of human hands," as they pointedly become God with us, then God in us. We behold the Body of Christ that we are. We pray to become the Body of Christ more and more.

Goffredo Boselli reminds us: "The end of the eucharistic body is the formation of the ecclesial body. Therefore there are two *epiclesis* that happen. The transformation of the bread and wine to the Body and blood of Christ is not, in fact, an end in itself; rather, the gifts are transformed so that those who eat them may become what they receive."

He goes on to say, "To receive communion is to be a communion."[7]

The particular words that we anticipate at each and every Eucharist speak of the church's historic understanding that the validity of the sacrament depends upon the substance used and the words offered, not the worthiness of the minister. But it makes a difference in the formation of the body if the people gathered can hear the words and receive each phrase rather than needing to hold the book in front of their eyes or rely on memory to know what is being said.

Words and substance may be all that is needed, but a true sense of awe and wonder is contagious. Slow it down. Lift the elements high. Hold them there for a moment so that all who are gathered can take it in. This is the Body of Christ. Behold.

And there's more.

It wasn't in a church building, but rather a classroom. The "altar" was a desk. John Westerhoff, teaching liturgy to Duke Divinity School students, began every class with a celebration of the Eucharist. By that time an Episcopalian for about seven years, I had participated in many eucharistic liturgies. But in this class, on this day, something happened at the fraction, the breaking of the bread. I had known a plate of wafers, but this day a single loaf of bread was being offered. (Westerhoff used to say that receiving communion in most churches required two acts of faith: first to believe that the wafers were bread, second to believe that the bread was the Body of Christ.)

Westerhoff lifted the blessed bread high and tore it in half. He then bent over the plate and slowly, methodically and silently, broke the bread into about thirty pieces, enough for every member of the class. There and then it hit me: The bread made from many grains becomes one. The one body then is broken for the many. I'd sung the hymn dozens of times:

> As grain, once scattered on the hillsides, was in this broken bread made one, so from all lands thy church be gathered into thy kingdom by thy Son. ("Father We Thank Thee Who Hast Planted," *The Hymnal 1982* #303)

On this day what I had known in my head became real in my heart: This is the Body of Christ, with whom we are one. This is the Body of Christ given for us. This is the Body of Christ, whom we become as we go forth from this place. Behold what you are.

The pace with which the words of the eucharistic rite are spoken and the clarity with which the actions are performed make a difference in the formation of the people gathered. So does the physical positioning of those who receive.

Standing or kneeling in the round (or oval or square) as space allows, so that we can receive communion alongside others, being able to see one another partake of the sacrament, able to see how varied we are in shape and size and stage of life, we grow season by season in our awareness of the body. Staying together until all have received deepens the experience. We are more likely to connect with others when in sight of one another. We take and eat, and witness to each other our humility and humanity.

As with so many body-building elements of the liturgy, such intimacy can seem easier to accomplish in a small or medium-sized church. The possibility of a more lingering distribution of the elements in a larger church setting depends on our ability to hold time and timing loosely.

One of our elders had a seizure during the Peace. A doctor and a nurse in the congregation went to her aid. A priest sat with the family anxiously nearby. Someone called 911, and we were told that an ambulance was on its way. We paused in our unknowing. The room was tight with sorrow, fear, love, and prayer.

The presider realized that the first responders would need room and access for a stretcher and other equipment. He announced calmly that we would move the liturgy outdoors for the Eucharist. We filed out of the church in silence and gathered by the outdoor altar. We sang and offered our gifts to God. The bread and wine were blessed. And when it was time for the distribution, we formed one large circle with the altar and one another. The community gathered as one body, elders identifying with the woman and her husband in the moment, small children not understanding, parents comforting their children, considering how to explain what was happening, what might happen. In that large circle we could share the experience, share our uneasiness, share our hope. Those who had been at that same outdoor altar on Easter day could remember that we gathered as the body in this way on that day, too. Even as we wondered what the outcome would be, we were given to enfold our wondering in Easter faith.

How we receive the body can profoundly shape our understanding of how we become the body.

How Can We Keep from Singing?

I arrived early for the Missional Voices conference at Virginia Seminary, so I stepped into the new chapel where I caught the end of the sparsely attended Friday Eucharist. Students were serving at the altar, dressed in cassock or alb, while a priest was reading the postcommunion prayer. Then, a hymn. I don't recall the hymn, although it was one I knew well. It was played on the organ with a sober, steady tempo. I don't worship with organ accompaniment very often, so this felt nostalgic. I also felt a little itchy for some verve.

The liturgy ended, and the altar party filed out somberly. As the credence table was cleared, a different group of students moved into the space. They came with guitars, drums, violin, microphones, and amplifiers. They started to practice music for the conference that was about to begin. They sang songs I'd never heard with a joy and energy that startled me. Throughout the following twenty-four-hour conference, the band led the singing at worship. I did not recognize a single song, but the students in the crowd sure did. And they sang with gusto.

Soon after the publication of *The Hymnal 1982*, the Episcopal Church realized a need to expand and diversify the music authorized for use in our worship. *Lift Every Voice and Sing II* in 1993 was quickly followed by *Wonder, Love, and Praise* in 1997, with both serving as supplements to *The Hymnal 1982*. In the preface to *Wonder, Love, and Praise*, the Standing Commission on Church Music wrote:

This supplement is . . . part of a continuing process of liturgical and musical enrichment and augmentation which offers an expanding vocabulary of spoken and sung prayer. The church has entered a new frontier of inclusive hospitality, not only in welcoming all to the table, but also in providing rites, forms, and music which encourage the sharing of one's cultural story to foster the unity proclaimed in the gospel. This supplement honors that pilgrimage and affirms "the participation of all in the Body of Christ the church, while recognizing our diverse natures as children of God."

In the years since, not only has the Episcopal Church moved to more fully embrace the diversity of the children of God, we have also embarked on a surge of missional enterprises, first planting churches with a goal of establishment, and then more recently, spawning a myriad of missional congregations and expressions.

As the Episcopal Church takes its twenty-first-century mission more and more to heart, so does our musical expression expand and diversify. This is not simply to appeal to a new generation or a new taste in music, but is a response to congregations bringing a diversity of culture and ethnicity to the church and to our new varied settings. New congregations are more likely to worship in spaces without organs, pews, stone floors, and high ceilings. New congregations are less likely to have English as their first language.

Singing is a powerful means for the expression and formation of a group, a collective. The secular world is aware of this. Patty Cuyler, codirector of Village Harmony, an organization that convenes community choirs around Chicago, observes, "In a chorus, it's not about overpowering another voice, but adjusting one's tune to create a harmony. It's the sum of the parts and the individuals don't count as much as what you do to make everyone sound good." Even the tourism website of Denmark, in promoting the practice of "corporate sing-alongs" in their business sector, claims, "Singing connects people socially and creates an invisible link— making participants move from an 'I-perspective' to an 'us-perspective.'"[8] Sports stadiums throughout the world swell with the sounds of many choruses. The stands actually hum through a game from start to finish, expressing and creating a shared spirit.

Similarly, singing in our liturgy cultivates a movement from "I" to "we," from individual Christian believer to the Body of Christ. How can we cultivate it? First, we can encourage people to sing out. The week-by-week welcome, printed or spoken, could include an encouragement: "When you sing, sing loudly." And perhaps add, "God loves to hear God's people sing, even if off key." Second, we can scatter the choir, if we have one, throughout the congregation for all hymns. Third, we can increase *a cappella* singing, with the instrumental accompaniment dropping out for a verse or two. As the congregation hears itself, and the sound is robust, the singing gains momentum. The simple act of singing a hymn then becomes one of the most body-building moments of the liturgy.

A Note about Perfection

At is best, the Sunday liturgy helps the participants experience a "foretaste of the heavenly banquet," to know more fully who they are as beloved creatures of God and what it is like to dwell in God's way. The church also serves to show the world how God wants human beings to live. This is a high calling. And it begs the question: If someone from "the world" were to come into our Sunday worship space, what would be revealed of the body we are growing into? What do we show of how human beings live in God's kingdom?

In some settings, the message that comes through is a high value of quality and perfection. We want to give our best to God, so we dress and behave accordingly. In this context, how we move, what we say, who sings and who doesn't, can all express this value. At the same time, uniform attire and movement by those who lead worship becomes part of the ritual action that offers stability and predictability. In other settings, the focus is on comfort, on "come as you are" or "you are welcome just as you are." All are welcome and little is expected, except, perhaps respect for others. Liturgy may have a homespun feel, and missteps are shrugged off, even enjoyed.

Both approaches are faithful, when the intention is understood by those participating in worship.

Perfection in worship can have the unintended effect of encouraging people to believe that they need to be equally perfect in the world. No one can sustain such perfection. And those who are far from perfect can feel unworthy or unwelcome in the liturgy. In 2020 when many churches started pre-recording much of the Sunday liturgy, the technology, lights, and cameras seemed to impose a call to perfection that surprised even most liturgically formal clergy. The near-perfect results were beautiful, but exacerbated the divide between what goes on in liturgy and what goes on in the living room of the observer.

Perfection in worship can also lead to worship of the worship rather than worship of God. Augustine guarded against this, saying, "when I find the singing itself more moving that the truth it conveys, I confess that this is a grievous sin. . . ."[9]

At the same time, a "come as you are" approach can too easily diminish the sacredness of a worship space and the worship that happens there. Sacred and profane can mix to the point that they are indistinguishable. Those who worship can be distracted by the seeming lack of care by those who are leading the worship. Respecting, setting apart some objects, some behaviors, and some words as holy can help us to realize the holiness of Christ, and to see that holiness in one another.

Earlier, I wrote of the need for balance in worship between representation of the immanence of God and the transcendence of God, as well as the need for balance between our individual experience of the liturgy and our communal experience of the liturgy. Here is yet another call for balance—a balance between perfection and anything goes, which is a balance, perhaps, between the sacred and the profane, between what we strive for and what we are. To strike this balance faithfully, we need to be mindful and aware of the purpose, function, and effect of what we are doing in the liturgy.

The Dismissal

> The Bishop, when present, or the Priest, may bless the people.

> The Deacon, or the Celebrant, dismisses them with these words . . . (BCP, 366)

If there were one word I might change in the rubrics, it would be "dismisses." I would change it to "sends forth" or "sends out." While the Latin root for dismiss, *missio*, is also the source of the word and concept of mission, "dismisses" carries too many connotations that do not apply to the work of the liturgy. In fact, none of them do. To dismiss is to (1) permit or cause to leave; (2) remove from position of service; (3) to reject serious consideration of; (4) to put out of judicial consideration, and to refuse to hear further in court.[10]

No wonder so many of us want to get back on our knees and pray again after we have been dismissed. To be sent, or sent forth, would more accurately describe and inspire what we are doing at this final point in the liturgy. For those who have been formed into the Body of Christ given for the world, this is a moment of anticipation. It is as if we have been preparing to become a doctor, a teacher, or a firefighter. Now we are ready for our commission— to do what we have been trained to do. Surely we do not feel ready yet. Will we really be able to do this thing that we have been prepared for?

Thankfully, as a church we are not being sent into the world alone. We are the body, and we are sent forth as the body. Appropriately, we do not respond to the sending forth alone; we respond together.

When the deacon says, "Let us go forth in the name of Christ" or, what would be an interesting alternative, "Let us go forth as the Body of Christ," a congregation formed to be the Body of Christ, given for the world, is going to know just how exciting and daunting that is. They will shout in unison, "Thanks be to God," and they may be so energized that they shout "Alleluia" at the end, even though it is not Eastertide. They may break out singing, in heart if not in voice, "From this place, to the world, we will go, hand in hand." The Body formed, the body sent.

To receive the Body of Christ is to become the Body of Christ. Not only in the eucharistic moment, but in all of the Sunday Eucharistic liturgy—the songs, the prayers, the movement—we have a profound opportunity to realize this transformation and identity.

Questions for Reflection

1. Can you identify ways in which your faith has been formed by the Sunday liturgies in your church?

2. Do you think of yourself as being part of the Body of Christ? If so, what does it mean to you?

3. Can you identify ways in which the Sunday liturgies of the church could strengthen that awareness and identity?

3 | Formed by Special Events and Seasonal Opportunities

We walked together, some carrying placards, others taking turns carrying the large cedar cross. Not a big crowd, twenty-five or so. Enough to been seen as intentional, enough to attract attention. I wore my collar and black cassock, signs of ministry, signs of the church. It was Good Friday, and we were walking the Way of the Cross through our town. For most of us, this was making church more public than usual. We felt a little timid and a little bold at the same time.

Somewhere between the fifth and sixth station, after we had passed the taqueria and before we reached the Interfaith Council building, a man rode by on his bicycle. "F*** God!" he yelled, waving his fist in the air. "F*** religion!" We walked on, changed.

Good liturgy both expresses what we believe and forms who we become. Because of that discomfiting encounter, those of us walking the Way of the Cross that Good Friday came to understand more fully a God made flesh, made vulnerable to the powers of this world. We came to understand more fully the gift of that vulnerability to us all. We understood a little better how it felt to claim our identity as Christians publicly, and what it means to be the Body of Christ in the world.

Baptism

It all starts with baptism. Baptism is a sacrament full of inward and spiritual grace. It is in baptism that we are united with Christ, that we are grafted onto the Body. We die with Christ; we rise with Christ. We are freed from the bonds of sin and of death. We are welcomed into the household of God. It is a big deal! How do we make it known? With a lot of celebration, and a lot of water.

The outward and visible sign of baptism is water. Full immersion in the waters of baptism was common for centuries, especially in warmer climates. Throughout the nineteenth century, though, when Victorian propriety and formality were in full bloom, baptisms became formal, private family affairs, and the practice of a light, symbolic, sprinkling of water evolved—for infants and adults alike.

Form followed function. A lot of the churches we worship in today were built in that Victorian era and in the century that followed. These churches were built with relatively small baptismal fonts in the back by the west door of the church, at the point of entry, or up by the pulpit, so that the family and clergy could easily gather around.

The liturgical renewal movement of the mid-twentieth century, however, caused Anglicans and other Christians to look back at our liturgical past, and to restore those practices that made liturgical and theological sense—baptism with a lot of water, for example. This is why the rubrics for baptism in the 1979 Book of Common Prayer state: "Each candidate is presented by name to the Celebrant, or to an assisting priest or deacon, who then immerses, or pours water upon, the candidate . . ." (307).

The death and resurrection imagery of baptism is especially visible in a baptism by immersion. The joy of resurrection becomes tangible at The Advocate through a variety of practices: The baptismal pool, in our case a large farm tub, is filled, ideally with water from the homes of all who have gathered, and is supplemented with water from the church's faucets. The whole congregation gathers round, ideally outdoors, with the children of the congregation at the water's edge, re-membering their own baptisms. The joy of witnessing the baptism reminds all who are gathered that this is a household event. It is an event by, for, and of the household of God.

Three times the one being baptized passes through the waters, in the name of the Father, and of the Son, and of the Holy Spirit.

In our baptism we die to the ways of sin, we die to all that would strive to separate us from God and from one another, and we die to the forces of wickedness that conspire to claim us. In our baptism we are born—born into Christ's resurrection, born into a life, and born into the Body of Christ, the church. The sealing oil can then be poured over the baptizand's head, and with the sign of the cross they are marked as Christ's own forever. Visual, sensorial, and tactile abundance makes the event more dramatic, more engaging, and more memorable.

The newly baptized is welcomed, the Peace of the Lord is shared, and the celebrant, using the pool as aspergillium, casts water upon the congregation, reminding them that they, too, are baptized. Abundance of water makes it plain. We are united by the waters of baptism and kindred in Christ. We have all emerged from the same womb; we have all passed through the same birthing waters; we have all become one body. We shout, "AMEN!" and sing, "There is one Lord, one faith, one baptism. There is one God who is Father of all."

After the Eucharist, the baptismal party is invited to the altar, where the newly baptized is presented with a candle to be lit on baptismal anniversaries ahead. Then the newly baptized, candle in hand (or in the hand of a godparent if need be), joins with the clergy and anyone else who processes forth. After the liturgy, there is cake, because cake is a symbol of celebration if ever there was one.

Baptism at its best is a memorable event, not only for the baptizand and for their household, but also for the household of God. Outward and visible signs help make it so. Sharing photos and celebrating baptismal anniversaries, as well as reciting the baptismal covenant on holy days throughout the year help keep the memory fresh. Baptism profoundly expresses and shapes what we believe about ourselves as baptized people, born again by water and the Spirit, the Body of Christ, given for the world.

The Holy Days and Seasons of the Year

From the expression and formation of the body in the movement of the Sunday liturgy, we start to see the expression and formation in the movement of the liturgical year. We go to church Sunday after Sunday, and we realize that we are going to church season by season as well, with each season proclaiming its own focus and calling. After a while, we discover that our sense of time is marked by our movement through Advent, Epiphany, and Easter, as well as through another summer, winter, or spring.

Liturgical seasons and the feast days that punctuate them provide abundant opportunities for expression and formation of the Body of Christ. Local traditions of seasonal and festival liturgies focus our attention on different aspects of our faith and life—anticipation, incarnation, Christ as a light to the world, penitence and forgiveness, resurrection, and ordinary times made holy. We mark the seasons with the liturgical colors of vestments, with collects that become familiar through the years, with certain hymns or service music, and perhaps with varying eucharistic prayers.

All of these good, rich practices foster faith and identity. Even so, many of our seasonal practices could benefit from a liturgical highlighter to underscore what we want to emphasize. As we anticipate an upcoming festival or season, before simply repeating what we have always done, we might pause and ask: How might the liturgy of this season, this day, more fully express and form the congregation as the Body of Christ? What elements of this season, this day, deserve special attention? How shall we highlight those elements? What music, what movements? How shall we use silence, if suggested? How can we best use our furnishings and our space? What more might we do to set this season apart from the season that precedes or follows? How will the people gathered be invited to experience the difference? How might we more fully engage the congregation? By what means will we inhabit these seasonal changes so that we feel it in our being?

We omit the Alleluias in Lent to denote the somber season that anticipates Easter joy. Each Sunday in Advent we sing "O Come O Come Emmanuel" so that the congregation associates that particular tune and those specific words with that season. What songs set apart and signify other seasons? Repetition is formational, and especially serves us well in the short seasons. What songs could be substituted as the song of praise in place of the Gloria during the season after Pentecost or for part of that exceptionally long season? What psalm, hymn, or other anthem might follow the readings beyond or in addition to the psalm of the day?

Could we play with rounds and canons, with a call and response that allows participants more fully to realize their part in the whole? Episcopalians/Anglicans relish "outward and visible signs" (the catechism's definition of sacraments). How might we use water, fire, incense, icons, and other art to imprint seasonal or festival connections? We are attuned to liturgical movement. Are there ways the altar party, or even the congregation, could move differently from one season to the next? Are there ways to augment the liturgical experience so that seasonal changes encourage the congregation's growing awareness of their identity as the Body of Christ?

Epiphany, All Saints, Holy Week, and Easter are especially rich with opportunities for the expression and formation of the Body of Christ.

Epiphany

In his 1997 book, *Christian Households*, Tom Breidenthal writes of the interplay between the individual households of the faithful, and the household of God, the church. He describes how our experiences of each of these households shape, form, and inspire the other. Church and home, back and forth. Any time we can connect the action and liturgy of the church to the action and liturgy of the home, the body is strengthened.

For example, during the Epiphany liturgy, a basket of chalk can be blessed and pieces distributed to each household for the marking, or chalking, of the lintel (top) of their home's door. Using chalk blessed at the church helps to make the connection between church and home. The *2018 Book of Occasional Services* (167) includes this blessing with directions:

> Loving God, bless this chalk which you have created, that it may be helpful to your people; and grant that through the invocation of your most Holy Name that we who use it in faith to write upon the door of our home the names of your holy ones Caspar, Melchior, and Balthazar, may receive health of body and protection of soul for all who dwell in or visit our home; through Jesus Christ our Lord. Amen.

Traditionally, the chalking is done above the lintel and takes this form: 20+C+M+B+[last two digits of current year]. The letters are the abbreviation for the Latin phrase *Christus mansionem benedicat*—"Christ bless this house." (A second meaning and mnemonic device is Caspar, Melchior, and Balthazar, the traditional names for the Magi.) The + signs represent the cross, and 20-21 is the year.

Church and home. What we learn and practice with sharing, caring, hospitality, boundaries, tolerance, forgiveness, and respect in one setting encourages our learning and practice sharing, caring, hospitality, boundaries, tolerance, forgiveness, and respect in the other. A piece of chalk is a trivial thing that can remind us of the connection between the household in which we live and the household of God that is the church. It is good to cultivate this connection!

It is the same for Candlemas, February 2, forty days after Christmas. On this feast day, we celebrate the presentation of the infant Jesus in the temple, where the old man Simeon declares Jesus to be a light to enlighten the nations. In time, Candlemas came to be celebrated as a festival of light—the light of Christ that burns in the church, in our homes, and in our hearts. The day can be marked with a candlelight procession and a blessing of candles to be taken home and used in the year ahead. Again, the *2018 Book of Occasional Services* (42–43) provides a guide:

> O eternal God, who have [*sic*] created all things; on this day you fulfilled the petitions of the just Simeon: we humbly ask you to bless and sanctify these candles for our use. Graciously hear our prayers and be merciful to us, whom you have redeemed by your Son, who is the light of the world, and who lives and reigns with you and the Holy Spirit, one God for ever and ever. Amen.

and

> O God, source of all light, today you revealed to the aged Simeon your light which enlightens the nations. Fill our hearts with the light of faith, that we who bear these candles may walk in the path of goodness, through Jesus Christ the Light of the World. Amen.

The themes of the season after Epiphany run rich. We hear the stories of God made known in Jesus, and we are invited to identify ourselves as the Body of Christ going out from the church into the world. Our traditional language for the season uses the image of the light of Christ scattering the darkness.

This language of light and darkness gives us an opportunity to become more mindful of the larger Body of Christ of which we are a part. First, the image of light going into the darkness doesn't resonate as clearly among our sisters, brothers, and siblings in the southern hemisphere, where the season coincides with summer and long hours of daylight. More important, our scripture and traditions of the season often imply that light is good and darkness is bad, even evil. As the Episcopal Church becomes more alert to the undercurrents of racism in our past and present, we are also becoming aware of the pain that the negative connotation of darkness can cause for our dark-skinned sisters, brothers, and siblings and about the division these implications perpetuate for us all.[11] Our identity as the Body of Christ given for the world can be strengthened when we intentionally change our language from darkness to shadows, from carrying the light of Christ into the world to carrying the love of Christ into the world.

To highlight the message of being sent forth as the Body of Christ, a smaller congregation might center the altar in the worship space. The presider could introduce the change by reminding those gathered that God is at the center. Rather than coming forward for the Eucharist, the people could remain standing in place as the altar party moves out from the center to distribute the sacrament among them. In some settings the people might administer the sacraments with reverence to one another. This reinforces the imagery of sharing Christ's love, as when we light the paschal candle from the new fire at the Easter Vigil and witness the fire going forth from that first flame.

Another way to highlight the sending forth of the Epiphany season is to commission one another for our life and work in the world. The 2018 *Book of Occasional Services* (154–155) includes the Recognition of Ministries in the Church and the World. The introduction says:

> The ministers of the Church are laypersons, bishops, priests, and deacons. Laypersons are commissioned for their ministry by the Sacrament of Holy Baptism, and no form of commissioning for special functions is necessary. The form that follows is intended for use when a public recognition of a special function is desired.

This rite is often used to commission laypeople for a variety of ministries in the church such as altar guild, ushers, and the vestry. What if each week of Epiphany, after the postcommunion prayer and before the blessing, the participants of various professions and vocations were called to stand before the congregation to be recognized for their work and ministries in the world, living out their baptismal commissioning, as artists, caregivers, merchants, bankers, first responders, teachers, students, and those who are in transition or retired?

An Epiphany Commission

All Those Engaged in Expressive
and Creative Endeavors

Presider: Now there are a variety of gifts but the same Spirit.

People: There are a variety of services but the same Lord.

Presider: We call forward all those engaged in expressive and creative endeavors.

*(Those to be commissioned come forward and present
themselves to the Presider and congregation.)*

Presider: Lord, we present to you these writers and poets, sculptors, painters and potters, performers and composers, those who build as well as those who design, and all who act to bring new things into being, mirroring God's own act of creation.

Commissioned: Here I am, Lord.

Presider: Do you celebrate your God-given gifts?

Commissioned: We do.

Presider: Do you seek the blessing of God and his church?

Commissioned: We do.

Presider: Do you promise, with the help of God, to use your gifts to serve God and neighbor?

Commissioned: We do.

Presider: Almighty God, you declare your glory and show forth your handiwork in the heavens and in the earth.

Commissioned: May we do the work you inspire and give us to in truth and beauty and for the common good.

Presider: Be ever present with your servants who seek through the arts to perfect the praises offered by your people on earth.

Commissioned: Open our eyes to behold your gracious hand in all your works and all our endeavors.

Presider: Almighty God, you have filled the world with beauty.

Commissioned: Grant us glimpses of your beauty and make us worthy to behold it unveiled for evermore.

Presider: May they rejoice and honor you in their acts of creation.

Commissioned: Grant us grace to honor you with our substance.

Presider: This we ask through Jesus Christ our Lord, who lives and reigns with you and the Holy Spirit, one God, forever and ever.

Commissioned: Amen.

Presider (addressing the congregation): We call forward all you, people of the church.

*(All who can come forward and lay hands
on those to be commissioned.)*

Presider: I present to you these members of the Body of Christ.

People: We celebrate your gifts and talents.

Presider: Will you, by your prayers and witness help these, our neighbors and friends, to share their gifts?

People: We will, with God's help.

Presider: Will you do all in your power to support these, our brothers and sisters, in their life in Christ?

People: We will, with God's help.

Presider: Do you witness this commissioning before each other, our community, and before God?

People: We do.

Together: We commission you to this work and pledge to you our prayers, encouragement, and support. May the Holy Spirit guide and strengthen you, that in this and in all things, you may do God's will in the service of Jesus Christ.

(All stand together before the Presider.)

Presider: There are varieties of activities.

Congregation: But the same God calls us to be faithful in what we do.

(The Presider offers the blessing to all, congregation returns to seats, procession, and an emphatic sending forth.)

When such a rite was used at The Advocate, one participant observed, "Though I see the secular work that I do in the world as a vocation and think of it as service to God's people, having my work commissioned by the church helped me to think about it in a new way. With the weight of the laying on of hands and the community sending me purposefully into the world to practice my profession, I began to see small moments where I could close the gap between Sunday church and an integrated Christian life."

Commissioning empowers and informs both those being commissioned and those who gather as witnesses. Commissioning acknowledges, blesses, and sends forth the people of the church to the ministries they hold in the world. It is in the spirit of sending forth that the Standing Commission on Liturgy and Music offered this "dismissal" for the conclusion of a liturgy to celebrate a new mission to the 74th General Convention of the Episcopal Church in 2003:

Our worship is ended. Our service in the world now begins. Go forth now in the name of Christ. Go into your own neighborhoods. Go to unknown lands and places. Go where God's name is well known and where it has yet to be known. Go to those who welcome you and to those who reject you. Go forth into the world and share the good news of God's love. Go in peace. Go in love. Go in joy. Alleluia! Alleluia![12]

Questions for Reflection

1. What aspects of the season after Epiphany are highlighted in the liturgy of the season in your church? What is the meaning of the season to you?

2. How does the church support and encourage your life and ministry in the world? Can you imagine practices that would allow you to experience that encouragement?

Holy Week

The powerful movement and symbolism of the entirety of Holy Week, as well as each liturgy in particular, invites further embodiment and formation, especially if we are able to take these liturgies out of our church buildings and into town. Holy Week begins on Palm Sunday with the Liturgy of the Palms and the procession that remembers Jesus's triumphal entry into Jerusalem, a very public event. According to Egeria, a pilgrim who wrote about Holy Week in fourth-century Jerusalem, the public enactment of the liturgy continued through the early centuries of the church:

> [A]s the eleventh hour approaches, the passage from the Gospel is read. . . . and the bishop immediately rises, and all the people with him, and they all go on foot from the top of the Mount of Olives, all the people going before him with hymns and antiphons, answering one to another: Blessed is He that cometh in the Name of the Lord. And all the children in the neighborhood, even those who are

too young to walk, are carried by their parents on their shoulders, all of them bearing branches, some of palms and some of olives, and thus the bishop is escorted in the same manner as the Lord was of old. For all, even those of rank, both matrons and men, accompany the bishop all the way on foot in this manner, making these responses, from the top of the mount to the city, and thence through the whole city . . . going very slowly lest the people should be wearied; and thus they arrive at the Anastasis at a late hour. And on arriving, although it is late, lucernare takes place, with prayer at the Cross; after which the people are dismissed.[13]

Sharing this story with the congregation can heighten awareness of our connection with the Body of Christ across the centuries. Remembrance of Jesus's triumphal entry into Jerusalem and Egeria's experience in the fourth century invites Christians today to go out into the streets and to gather at the entrance of our town or city. There we can more viscerally hear the story of Jesus, the colt, the people, and the palms. Standing on the street or gathering on our church's lawn, we too can wave our palm branches or flowers brought from our own gardens and trees (the equivalent of palms in first-century Jerusalem). Long stalks of bamboo are especially dramatic. The processional cross on Palm Sunday symbolizes Jesus, and we want to be as close to him as we can.

When basketball champions return to the college campus, people throng and cheer. Participants in twenty-first-century marches and rallies carry placards and shout chants. A contemporary procession might include a call with an echo response: "Blessed is the One who comes in the name of the Lord!" or "We are the people of God!" Placards that proclaim, "Sight to the blind!" or "Jesus saves" or simply "Hosanna!" strengthen the connection between the familiar rallies and parades of our day and the amassing of crowds in first-century Jerusalem.

Singing in a procession outdoors is problematic. For those who really want to sing, a simple repetitive chorus is more likely to hold the procession together than a complex hymn. "Hosanna Glory, Hosannah" (a variation of the Anders Nyberg arrangement of the South African hymn, "Jesus is coming") can follow "Jesus is coming, oh yes I know." "Hosanna, Hosanna, We're Going to See The King" set to the Andrae Crouch tune "Soon and Very Soon, We Are Going to See The King" works well too.

Jesus, represented by the cross and crucifer (the person carrying the cross), advances along the way as the people wave and cast branches, flowers, and even garments (it's biblical!) before him. The procession halts for the Collect at the Door, the crucifer walks over the scattered branches and garments, and the congregation follows into the church for hymns, readings, prayers, and Eucharist.

The reading of the Passion provides a glaring contrast to the exuberance of the earlier blessing of the palms and joyful procession. It also serves as a gateway to the profound mysteries enacted and embodied in the liturgies of Holy Week—Maundy Thursday, Good Friday, and the great Vigil of Easter—otherwise known as the Triduum. To emphasize this threshold, some congregations postpone the reading of the Passion so that it follows the Eucharist and a post-communion hymn. Thus the reading concludes the Palm Sunday liturgy, which ends in silence, underscoring the reality that we are moving into a drama together.

The story of Maundy Thursday evokes a more intimate setting than the other liturgies of Holy Week, as Jesus gathers with his disciples "in the upper room." So much happens on this night—the institution of the Eucharist in that last supper, the foot-washing, the giving of the New Commandment (*mandatum*, from which the day gets its name), and in many churches, the stripping of the altar.

For the people of The Advocate, Maundy Thursday evokes our most full realization of ourselves as the Body of Christ, called to serve. Distinct from the other liturgies of Holy Week that take place publicly in town or on church property, Maundy Thursday happens in a rustic lodge at a camp outside of town. This setting not only causes us to identify with the disciples who gathered with Jesus in a place set apart, it also creates for us an awareness of the church, the body, within the world, yet distinct from it.

An intern noted, "On Maundy Thursday, when I require my GPS to guide me to the secluded place where the faithful are gathering, there is a sense of being a community set apart from the world, one that knows a disruptive secret. The change in setting, and the need for all hands to help with set up, serving, and take down reminds us that the work of the church is countercultural and requires us each to participate."

The congregation sits at round tables of eight with a member of the vestry or other lay leader assigned as a table servant. The mood of the occasion is festive, joyful, sweet, and convivial.

We gather singing as the story of the Exodus is read aloud. The blessings for the agape meal in the *Book of Occasional Services* (84) are read, and the food and drink are served. At the conclusion of the meal, the table servants clear everything except for the chalice, paten, and flowers. They bring in tubs of warm water, towels, and sponges, and we hear the story from the Gospel of John of Jesus washing the feet of his disciples. At each table, a chair is designated for the foot washing, and all are invited to take turns sitting in that chair to have their feet washed. There is no pressure to participate. But even the shy or reserved among us, following a shared meal together, are likely to come forward to be served and to serve.

A homily follows the foot washing. We pray, we sing, we exchange the Peace. Then we share in the Eucharist. Each chalice and paten is brought forward, and bread and wine are blessed. The table servants carry the consecrated bread and the wine to those at their table, and each in turn serves another. The people of the body serve and are served in the intimate communion of their table and within the community of the many gathered in the room. The evening ends with the clearing of "the altar"—the flowers, the bread, the wines, the color, and the beauty that have marked the evening are taken away. We gather on the porch by the light of the full or nearly full moon and sing, "Jesus, remember me, when you come into your kingdom." We hear the story of Jesus in the garden with his sleeping disciples from the twenty-sixth chapter of the Gospel of Matthew.

"Through our participatory experience of this liturgy," one young adult of The Advocate observed, "each of us is able to embody the disciples' experience of a care-full community in the midst of uncertainty." We serve and are served, we love and are loved.

We depart in silence.

In addition to the Good Friday liturgy of the Book of Common Prayer and the Way of the Cross described at the start of this chapter, another embodied Good Friday tradition of The Advocate is the Good Friday Wake, which is easily adapted to homes or a church site. It originated in the familiar experience of the gathering of family and friends following a death.

The day after my grandmother died, my family gathered from near and far. Late afternoon and into the evening, sitting in her kitchen and living room, we talked. Plenteous coffee, a bottle of wine, cold cuts, and coffee cake fed the conversation as we discussed the funeral plans. We shared memories and stories, we laughed about her personality quirks, we sighed about our experiences of her support and care, and we reminded ourselves of the wisdom she had given us. My grandmother's body was not with us in the house, but her spirit was there.

Decades later, a beloved parishioner died on a Thursday afternoon. A meeting was scheduled at The Advocate that night. But given our sorrow, the meeting was cancelled, and we gathered in the chapel for a vigil instead. Evening Prayer served as a guide as we read scripture, prayed the Litany at the Time of Death, and shared memories and stories of our beloved friend. We laughed at the phrases he had used and reminded ourselves of the ways he had inspired us. We mourned together and were comforted by our shared memories and shared loss.

These gatherings are not unusual. They happen in every faith tradition, and in families and households everywhere. Jewish people have a custom of "sitting shiva" for seven days of mourning, praying, and sharing. Perhaps Mary and her friends sat shiva when Jesus died, if only for a day or two. . . .

Many Christians keep a vigil through the night between the Maundy Thursday liturgy and noon on Good Friday. This custom developed from the story of Jesus's response to his disciples when they fell asleep in the Garden of Gethsemane in the hours before his arrest: "So, you could not stay awake with me one hour?" The vigil is traditionally held at an "altar of repose," which is sometimes decorated with flowers. One or more of the faithful attend to the reserved sacrament, praying quietly during assigned hours through the night and into the early morning.

A Good Friday Wake is of another order and serves a different purpose. Sometime in the evening friends and family are invited to gather. As with any wake, the atmosphere is a blend of somber and cheery, a blend of sacred and simple fellowship. And as with any wake, food is on hand, which might be hot tea and hot cross buns or soup and bread. Those gathered are invited to sit around a large table, or in chairs set up in circle, and share memories or stories about Jesus. Some recount Jesus as he is revealed in scripture, while others speak about how he has been revealed to them through sacrament or personal prayer. Periods of silence interrupt the conversation.

Out of the shared experience, stories spark stories, evoking memories that evoke further memories. Reflecting on the feeding of the multitude, one person might ask, "Do you remember that time when he wanted us to try to feed that whole crowd of people who'd gathered to hear him preach?" Another continues, "He asked us,

'What have you got?'" and then adds reflectively, "He used to ask us that a lot. . . ." Or, one person said, "I guess the first time I met Jesus was as a kid in church camp. He asked me to be his partner to throw water balloons! I always remember he was so kind. . . ."

Some of these stories are prepared by the facilitators ahead of time as a means to encourage participation, but most emerge spontaneously among those gathered. Feeling at once shy and bold, hesitant and faithful, we share our stories. At the toll of a bell, a period of silent meditation and reflection is indicated, before another period of conversation begins. People sit or stand, walk about, get some tea, visit an icon, come and go. It is important that people know they are free to leave at any time, unselfconsciously. Despite awkward moments, formational in their own way, the structure falls away into silence and comment, silence and prayer. The facilitator draws the Wake to a close, saying: "I remember Jesus, who said, 'Where two or three are gathered in my name, I am there in the midst of them.' Let us pray together the prayer he taught us: Our Father in heaven. . .".

The Wake ends with a refrain from the Good Friday liturgy: "We adore you O Christ and we bless you, because by your Holy Cross, you have redeemed the world." And then, "I remember Jesus, who said, 'Peace I leave with you; my peace I give you.' Let us share with each other a sign of Christ's peace." The Peace is exchanged, and the gathered head out into the night.

A Good Friday Wake requires committed leadership and modeling by the facilitator(s). Imagination, an openness to sharing personal experience, a generosity of spirit, and hospitality are all essential ingredients. A listening presence is as integral as the willingness to speak. For those who find meaning in this ritual, the Wake brings the story alive and is an opportunity to experience the incarnation of Jesus in a new way. "This was folk theology," one participant said, "a community of faith doing theology together, in the most amazing way. . . . It's been very hard for me to remember, all day, that it's not Easter yet—not because, sitting around the icon, we forgot that we were grieving a departed friend, but because in our shared grieving and remembering, that friend became so real and present to me."

Questions for Reflection

1. As you consider the liturgies of Holy Week, what are the practices of your church that carry particular meaning for you? What is that meaning?
2. Are there ways in which the congregation can be more engaged in the expression or meaning of each of the liturgies of Holy Week in order to better understand themselves as the Body of Christ given for the world?

Easter

Beginning with the Great Vigil of Easter, the fifty days of the Easter season insist upon liturgy that shouts the conquering of sin and death, and that joyously proclaims the way of freedom and life. This is the way of the Body of Christ.

It begins with the Great Vigil of Easter. Words and movement emphasize the four stations of the night: fire, word, water, and altar. On this night, the Body of Christ, a body alive in the power and hope of the Resurrection is vividly, tangibly realized. Death and the ways of the world no longer have dominion. We gather in darkness, feeling the tomb, subdued by its power and force. Then come a spark and flame. The new fire is lit.

To experience the light of Christ bursting into and through the darkness of death, the people gather around the fire as *it* bursts into life. Make the fire as substantial as the setting allows so that the congregation can watch the light spread from fire to candle, to candle, to candle, to candle, and feel the exultation swell. Keep the candles lit for as long as possible to experience the literal illumination of the Word that follows. Create an atmosphere conducive to the telling of ancient story. As the setting allows, find ways to engage the congregation in the story itself, with words or sounds, listening attentively for their cue. At St. Christopher's Church in Havelock, North Carolina, the congregation tips rain sticks during the telling of the Flood story.

After the stories, the focus of the Vigil shifts to baptism. An abundance of water, whether or not a baptism is scheduled, encourages all who are baptized to be reminded that we have died with Christ and have risen with Christ. It is by baptism that we are one with Christ. Through baptism we have become members of the Body that we behold in the bread of the Eucharist. This is something to shout about. Asperge the people generously. Consider including a procession with a resurrection icon and a singing of Alleluias before a turn to the altar.

From the Paschal shout through the sending forth, let there be both solemn joy and revelry. Sing, or even dance, the ancient Easter troparion:

Christ is risen from the dead,
trampling down death by death,
and upon those in the tomb,
bestowing life.

Consider actual foot stomping for the second line. Consider raising arms at the last. Consider repeating the troparion to conclude the liturgies throughout the season.

Carry the waters of baptism through the season, too. Let Eastertide be the season of re-membering our baptism. After the opening acclamation, include with the "song of praise" a blessing of the water and asperges of the people:

Presider: Almighty God, who through the water of baptism has raised us from sin into new life, and by the power of your life-giving Spirit ever cleanses and sanctifies your people: + Bless, we pray you, this water for the service of your holy church; and grant that it may be a sign of the cleansing and refreshment of your grace; through Jesus Christ our Lord.

All: Amen.

Presider: I saw water proceeding out of the temple, from the right side it flowed.

All: And all those to whom that water came shall be saved. Alleluia.

(*As the presider asperges the people all sing.*)[14]

There is nothing like water on the nose and eyeglasses to secure memory and to engage a person in the liturgy.

All Saints

The Feast of All Saints (November 1) falls at the end of Ordinary Time each year and offers a profound opportunity for expression and formation of the Body of Christ. On this festival day we reflect on the witness of those who have died in the faith of the church. In prayer and song, we remember all the saints, "who from their labors rest."

Traditionally, the Feast of All Saints is the day we remember the saints with a capital *S*, those who have been recognized by the church for their faithful life and death. The next day, November 2, through the Commemoration of all Faithful Departed, we are encouraged to remember saints with a small *s*, those who have inspired us personally—parents and godparents, teachers, clergy, mentors, and more.

The two remembrances are frequently conflated in celebration the Sunday following the Feast of All Saints, known as "All Saints Sunday." Although distinctions between the capital *S* saints and the small *s* saints are ecclesiastically significant, the blending of the two is inspiring and pastorally kind. As the secular world recognizes and adapts the Mexican celebration of the Day of the Dead more routinely—in schools, public libraries, and homes—it is apparent that we all yearn to remember our ancestors in family and in love, as well as in the life of our faith.

The names of the faithful departed are commonly read in the context of the Prayers of the People, or in the body of Eucharistic Prayer D, Rite II. Large congregations hear the names of those who have died in the past year. Small churches can more readily invite the names of all the deceased who are remembered in heart and mind.

Another practice is to invite members of the congregation to bring images, icons, or photographs of the deceased who have formed or inspired their life and faith. These images and icons are placed around the worship space, some resting against a wall or on non-sacred furnishings, others attached to hanging ribbons. Surrounded by the cloud of witnesses, the people worship. Throughout the liturgy, eyes drift to a favorite "Saint"—Julian of Norwich or Francis of Assisi—and to a favorite "saint"—a grandfather or an encouraging mentor. One person sees a beloved uncle next to the beloved grandmother of another, next to a renowned saint of the church. This is the Body of Christ. We are the Body of Christ.

At The Advocate, after the liturgy, we share a table fellowship with one another. The people are encouraged to prepare dishes from recipes of a beloved saint; "Ellen's turkey tetrazzini" is an All Saints favorite. And we share stories—one woman points to a photo of her daughter who died young and tells of her love and joy; another points to a photo of Dietrich Bonhoeffer and tells the story of his faith even in prison. These images and narratives inspire us to live the life of faith together.

Another meaningful practice is to begin the liturgy on All Saints Sunday with a Litany of Saints. Ours was adapted from one written for Church of the Holy Family in Chapel Hill in the 1990s. As the names of the saints are chanted, the congregation responds to each grouping with "Stand here beside us!" It is a long litany, listing a hundred saints or more, grouped in categories of their way of life or death. As each name or cluster of names in chanted, the congregation chants, "Stand here beside us!" "Stand here beside us!" The church soon resounds with the presence of them all.

> ... Holy ones who died in witness to the Christ: Stand here beside us.

> Stephen the deacon, the first martyr, stoned in Jerusalem: Stand here beside us.

> Justin, Ignatius, and Polycarp, who refused the incense to Caesar: Stand here beside us.

> Thomas Cranmer, Hugh Latimer, and Nicholas Ridley, burned in Oxford: Stand here beside us.

> James Reeb, Jonathan Daniels, Viola Liuzzo, shot in Alabama: Stand here beside us.

> Michael Schwerner, Medgar Evers, shot in Mississippi: Stand here beside us.

> Martin Luther King, shot in Memphis: Stand here beside us.

> Janani Luwum, shot in Kampala: Stand here beside us.

> Oscar Romero, shot in San Salvador: Stand here beside us.

The litany ends with a collect, and a breaking forth of the singing of that peerless hymn, "For All the Saints."

This practice can be adapted online, chanting "Let us stand beside you," with images of the saints crossing the screen during the litany, and images of the saints crossing the screen while a virtual choir sings "For All the Saints."

The heavenly host surely surrounds us each and every Sunday when we gather. But on this day, with their images among us and their names chanted or remembered in prayer, we are given a powerful reminder of their presence still with us, the faithful cloud of witnesses, an integral part of a communion, the church, a Body, far greater and more populated than the one we see and greet Sunday by Sunday.

By means of this powerful imagery, we join in the Great Thanksgiving with angels and archangels, and all the company of heaven singing Holy, Holy, Holy, knowing that we are not in this life alone. Far from it.

Lesser Feasts

There are other feasts of the church year that can express and form our faith. The Feast of St. Francis, celebrated on or about October 4, has become a day for the popular public blessing of the animals, which provides a playful and sweet connection between the household of the church and the household of home. St. Blaise Day on February 3 can be a day to pray for good health and for protection against the flu and other viruses. Two candles are crossed under a person's chin while a simple prayer is offered:

> May you be delivered from all illnesses of the throat and any other ailments. In the Name of the Father, and of the Son, and of the Holy Spirit. Amen.

This can make for a meaningful public offering as well. Recipients can be sent home with two candles to burn through the winter.

Ember days are known primarily by clergy who as candidates for ordination were required to write to the bishop at that time. Ember days can also serve as a time for lay vocational reflection and for recognition of lay ministries in the world. The priest and available lay leaders might arrange to meet with lay members on Ember days at their place of work and affirm that work by their presence.

Lesser known rogation days can be used for celebrating the earth and its fruits and those who work in the fields. These are good days simply to offer the prayer for agriculture in the Book of Common Prayer or to invite the congregation to watch a video about farm-workers. Recommended possibilities include the 1960 Edward R. Murrow film *Harvest of Shame*, its 2010 update *Harvest of Dignity*, or the 2020 film *Stories Beyond Borders*. A parish-wide project at Grace Episcopal Church in Waynesville, North Carolina included compiling photos or videos from one another's gardens, the local farmers market, and farmsteads throughout the county. The ensu-ing online video served to bring the congregation together and also helped them to see their place in the wider community.

For Agriculture

Almighty God, we thank you for making the earth fruit-ful, so that it might produce what is needed for life: Bless those who work in the fields; give us seasonable weather; and grant that we may all share the fruits for the earth, re-joicing in your goodness; through Jesus Christ our Lord. *Amen.* (BCP, 824)

Liturgy in Time of Crisis

Throughout the liturgical year, unsettling events of our community or events of the world around call us to be together and to gather for prayer and for comfort. The church must be ready for these moments of trauma of the collective psyche, and to provide a gathering time, place, and liturgy.

September 11, 2001, was such an occasion. As the horrific events of the morning unfolded, we did not know how many had died or who had died or who was responsible or what would happen next. We did know that as a people our nation had been attacked, and that we were in a state of shock and of grief. We wanted to be with those we loved. At Church of the Holy Family in Chapel Hill, North Carolina, where I was serving as a priest on staff, we knew we needed to be together that evening as church. Clergy and lay leadership gathered and prayed for wisdom, insight, and faithfulness, then prepared a liturgy with prayers, readings, hymns, and the Eucharist. We realized we were "in the midst of things we cannot understand" (the Burial rite); we realized our place in the biblical story of betrayal, exile, and healing; and we realized our oneness with one another and with God. However unpolished our liturgy may have been in the immediacy of our need, the liturgy expressed our faith and formed it profoundly.

Sometimes we do this liturgical remembering in a public space.

A Haiti Remembrance

A companion relationship with a small church in Haiti brought home to us the 2010 earthquake in Port au Prince. We wanted to use the first anniversary of that earthquake to remember and pray for those who had perished, and for those whose lives were forever changed. Acknowledging that most of those who died had been simply going about their lives in the public square in Port-au-Prince, we decided to gather outdoors in a place of business and commerce in our own town. We were aware that by doing so we would again bear public witness to our God, who is with us in times of darkness and despair. So we chose a popular lawn in front of a nearby market. We invited our sponsoring churches to join us and posted flyers around town.

We gathered a few minutes before the time of the earthquake the previous year. We surrounded ourselves with enlarged 8x10 photos from the earthquake and with handiwork brought home from mission trips to Haiti. We stood in silence. Then we began to pray a litany:

> Throughout our holy scriptures, God promises mercy and deliverance from misery and disaster. . . .

A security guard then approached us, calling out, "Who's in charge here?" The people gathered looked from him to me. "I am," I replied as boldly as I could. "This is private property," he proclaimed even more boldly. "You can't do this here." "We are here to remember the earthquake in Haiti," I said. By now we were getting more attention from the market's customers than I anticipated. "It doesn't matter," he said to hold his ground. "You can't do it here." I pointed to the photos. I said, "We are here because the earthquake happened as people were going to their markets in Haiti that day. They were out in public when the earthquake hit." He gazed at the photos. "Besides," I said, "we will only be here about ten more minutes." "Please," I said, "let us stay ten minutes to remember the people of Haiti. You can join us if you'd like." The guard agreed and stood about ten feet away, watching and listening. Others watched from their picnic tables or the sidewalk visibly moved, even approving of what we were about. We continued the litany:

Let us pray for the church and the people of Haiti. . . .

At 4:53 we tolled a bowl bell for thirty-five seconds. We stood in further silence, and then prayed the Lord's Prayer in Haitian Creole.

Afterwards, we agreed that being out in public, rather than in a church building, made the experience of all more real. The tolling of the bell made us poignantly aware of how quickly the earthquake changed the lives of so many who were simply going about their daily lives when it happened.

We made a public witness that day. Again, it was a little scary. Again, we were challenged, and made to feel bold when we had not expected to be. Again, we were and we became the Body of Christ.

During the Covid-19 pandemic of 2020–21, such a public gathering was not possible. Thankfully, we were able to gather online, and through readily accessible technology we could see and hear each other. We shared our sorrow over what we had lost by being required to keep physical distance, wear masks, and stay at home. We missed the Eucharist, our common singing, the joy of gathering in a space we love. Still, we heard the words of our faith and we prayed together. Particularly compelling was the prayer written and prayed by the faithful in the midst of a pandemic a hundred years before, the traditional language making it all the more time-transcending:

> O Most mighty and merciful God, in this time of griev-
> ous sickness, we flee unto thee for succor. Deliver us, we
> beseech thee, from our peril; give strength and skill to all
> those who minister to the sick; prosper the means made
> use of for their cure; and grant that, perceiving how frail
> and uncertain our life is, we may apply our hearts unto that
> heavenly wisdom which leadeth to eternal life; through
> Jesus Christ our Lord. Amen. (BCP 1928, 45)

In the regular practice of adjusting the liturgy to the day or the season or the people gathered, something formational happens. Through the weekly sharing of the Prayers of the People and the seasonal practices such as walking the Way of the Cross on Good Friday and the Epiphany commissions, the faithful are prepared for crises that require particular liturgies to express and contain emotions of unexpected fear, grief, and sorrow. Through these practices, we learn how to be open and honest with God and with one another. We grow to understand that worship and liturgy are the means by which we are formed in faith and express who we are and what we believe.

Liturgy for the Fun and Formation of It

Liturgy can be fun as well as formative. The blessing of homes, pets, or backpacks remind us that God is present in all places and that wherever we go and whatever we do, we carry within us our identity as the Body of Christ. The meaning of blessing is to be emphasized on these occasions, the setting apart of that which is to be singled out by God's presence, God's grace, and God's peace.

Anniversaries are wonderful opportunities to celebrate, to remember, and be re-formed. The anniversary of the birth of a particular church can be marked with stations for every year, decade, or century. Old customs, such as "beating the bounds," can become new traditions. At The Advocate we have done it twice, five years apart. The idea is to remind everyone of the boundaries of the parish, and also to make sure those boundaries are in order. We gather by the pond, stoke the thurible (the metal censer suspended from chains, in which incense is burned during worship services), pull a bucket of water from the pond for spraying the boundaries with a dipped branch (an asperges), and pray:

> O God, as our prayers go up with the incense, we pray your blessings on this water, that as it flows from pond to pitcher, and flies from holly branch to leaves and grass and pine needles, it would be a sign for us of your abundant blessing. Amen.

From there we walk to the mailbox by the road, where we stop and pray:

> O God, you know we need boundaries, definite times and places in which to seek you and be found by you, to get better acquainted, to dream dreams, and to make future plans. O God, thank you for the gift of this land. Today we beat its bounds to banish fear and hatred, cowardice and complacency. Today we sow seeds of passion for justice, solidarity with the displaced, and love for the earth. Make us forceful and fruitful. Give us a good harvest. Through Jesus Christ. Amen.

We began our circumnavigation.

This wasn't to claim the land as "ours" but more to bless the land and set it apart for God's purposes and God's delight. The land had been there much longer than we had. The Occaneechi band of the

Saponi Nation dwelled across the region for centuries, and the pond we cherish had been fished by locals for generations. We were simply the next stewards, and it was now our calling to tend the land, to share the land with others, to be strengthened and inspired by it. Like so much that is "church," the land was given to us to encourage faithful practice. After five years, the congregation's pacifist proclivities recommended a change of nomenclature from "beating the bounds" to "touching the bounds" when we repeated the circuit. As with liturgy, repetition reminds. At best, even playful liturgies remind us that as the Body of Christ, we are given for the world. If we are to steward a site for a season, we are stewards on behalf of others as well as for ourselves.[15]

Questions for Reflection

1. How have you experienced a church liturgy beyond Sundays, weddings, funerals, and the proscribed holy days of the year?

2. How did that liturgy help to shape your identity as a member of the Body of Christ?

3. Can you think of events or occasions in the life of the church that would be fun to celebrate in the context of a liturgy and would also be formative?

4 | Liturgy of a Church without a Church Building

The head of the altar guild reserved the trunk of her car for large plastic tubs, carefully organized with chalices, patens, linens, and candles. Sunday after Sunday, she carried the tubs from her car into the worship space to set up the altar. Everything else—the processional cross, water coolers, folding tables, worship guides, and name buttons—was stowed week by week in a 5x8 cargo trailer in my driveway. On Sunday it was readied for the 10-mile drive to the space we rented for our worship. There, volunteers waited to unload the trailer and set up church.

After the first year, we changed locations and were given access to a closet. This reduced the loading and unloading, but not the setting up and taking down. We still had no place to put a sign. "My kingdom for a sign," I would say. "How will people know where to find us?" I had an 18x36-inch magnet with the church logo and website address on the side of my car, and I promised my ten-year-old daughter that we would have a church sign somewhere else by the time she turned fourteen (we barely made that deadline). In our fifth year, we signed a lease for an office and small meeting space in town. Now we had storage space, a meeting space, and a sign, but not for Sundays.

Having church without a church building is both adventurous and wearisome. In the early years of The Advocate, we didn't even think about going online. In 2003, there were no smartphones, Facebook pages, or YouTube videos.

We were challenged by finding a location, negotiating agreements with the owner of the building, calculating how to adapt church practices to the space, setting up and taking down the church week after week, and designing signs, banners, and a car magnet. It was said that The Advocate was the Brigadoon of musical fame, appearing out of the mist each week, then disappearing again.

At first there was genuine excitement. Here's a space—how shall we organize worship here? Which way should we place the chairs? Do we bring a box of prayer books, use service guides, or perhaps tablets? How do we cover what is already on the walls? Or should we just let them be? For a while, The Advocate rented space from a Unity church, where one wall was covered in mirrors, forcing half the congregation to crane their necks to avoid their own reflections. We added the hanging of large swaths of cloth over the wall of mirrors to the setup tasks each week.

Early on, we were determined to rent space with movable chairs rather than pews, and with a piano rather than an organ. This would give us flexibility in music and the arrangement of space and would also allow us to face one another. Rather than using bound copies of the Book of Common Prayer and *The Hymnal 1982*, we used three-ring binders as our prayer book and hymnal. This allowed us to change rites and prayers from one season to the next, using prayers from the Book of Common Prayer, *Enriching Our Worship* and, with the permission of our bishop, occasional prayers from elsewhere in the Anglican Communion. The binders also allowed us to include hymns from *The Hymnal 1982*; *Lift Every Voice and Sing II*; *Wonder, Love, and Praise*; Taizé; St. Gregory of Nyssa in San Francisco; and other public domain songs without purchasing or storing hundreds of books. We quickly learned the ways of copyright permission, RiteSong, and One License, recording the source of every song we copied and reporting which songs were sung when. Importantly, the binders made the liturgy more user friendly, with all the rites, readings, and prayers in one book and in sequential order.

We decided not to have weekly bulletins. Page numbers for the liturgy could be announced and other announcements could be shared in church and by email. This eliminated the cost of paper and production time. As we embraced the identity of a "new old" church, we wrestled with when to lean into the new and when to embrace the old. We determined not to use PowerPoint and a screen because we believed that twenty-first century people had enough of that in their lives already. We wanted people to be invited into a space that had a more natural, authentic, and maybe even a retro feel.

Every rented worship space has its advantages and disadvantages. We rented from a synagogue for five years, which prompted us to dig deeper into the Hebrew scriptures, learn about Jewish customs and high holy days, and prepare food for our shared meals according to kosher guidelines. The building was built for a Bible Church in the 1960s, and the actual worship space was basically a brick box with a linoleum floor and several hundred red plastic chairs. Bookcases full of bound copies of the Torah covered one wall, while another featured the Ark that contained the Torah scrolls. Beside the Ark was an American flag, a symbol cherished by the Holocaust survivors of their congregation. Rather than place our processional cross in front of these existing symbols, we oriented our worship on the east-west axis. To create our own setting, we suspended seasonal hangings on a large canvas backdrop, hung from the ceiling panels. This, too, was part of the routine of setting up and taking down church every Sunday.

It was the setup and takedown that grew wearisome. The Advocate rented worship space for eleven years. Fifty-two Sundays a year, with two liturgies every Sunday for six of those years, we set up and took down our church more than eight hundred times. Unpacking those binders, week after week, I imagined what it would be like to have a church building, where books could be left in little racks on the backs of pews throughout the week. How wonderful it would be to have a place to keep our vestments. I stopped wearing a cincture (a rope worn around the waist) in those years because it got caught in my car door every time I carried too much into the building at a time. I shudder to think about how many times a stole fell to the ground.

We simplified vestments. Acquiring albs (white robes) in all sizes for lay ministers was prohibitively expensive, and storage was not available. Thus, only the clergy wore albs, except at the Easter Vigil, when we would borrow vestments from the closets of neighboring churches for the crucifer, gospel bearer, the thurifer (who carries the thurible), and the cantor.

Our setup and takedown was labor intensive. We opted to do all that we could to transform our rented space for Christian liturgical sacramental worship. Without the architectural and aesthetic assistance of a building designed for such worship to remind us that God is indeed out there and beyond us, even as God is with us where we are, we had to create our own reminders of transcendence to call us upward and outward. We used the Tibetan bowl bell with its lingering toll at the start of the liturgy, in the moments of the eucharistic prayer when we joined our voices with all the company of heaven (the *Sanctus*), and when the elements were lifted by the celebrant. Crucifers were encouraged to carry the cross high, in an attempt to draw our eyes heavenward. We decided early on to spend scarce resources to commission a hand-carved processional cross, which would give us a thing of beauty in what might otherwise be a plain or distracting setting. Beauty calls us beyond the here and now.

All of these practices meant that plenty of "stuff" needed to be set up every Sunday. To make it happen in a relatively short period of time required many volunteers. As a result, we attracted people who like to be involved. One visitor said that during our setup, we looked like a Montessori classroom, with people all tending to one task or another.

There were others who complained: "I sometimes just want to come to church and sit and not feel guilty if I don't do something." Try as we might to say that was okay, the culture of The Advocate said otherwise. We were a thoroughly engaging congregation—engaging with God, with the community, with one another, and with something new. We had a lot of energy and there was a lot to be done. This meant that we were also off balance.

The church and its liturgy cannot be about "doing" all the time. We all have seasons of our lives when we are too overwhelmed by life to actively engage, even to stand and sing. Sometimes we simply need to be in church and let the liturgy wash over us. It wasn't until The Advocate settled into a building of our own that the balance between tasking and being began to emerge. We then included in the welcome each Sunday that some who are present may need to just be. Even so, we asked that as members of the body gathered, they still try to be attentive to the Spirit of God moving within and among us all.

Questions for Reflection

1. Do you experience yourself as a do-er or a be-er in church?
2. What would help you to experience a balance between the two?

In my young adult life, Anglo-Catholic mentors taught me the value of "giving our best to God" in the liturgy: fabulous vestments, sung Masses, dressing up for church, and more. In secular or rented transient space, though, it can be challenging to "rejoice in the splendor of the beauty of holiness." It can be difficult to find a balance in the expression of the immanence and transcendence of God. Liturgy that is not in a church building requires a particular attentiveness to the formation of the Body of Christ. It becomes all the more important to encourage participation of the people in the liturgy. Participation fosters focus and formation.

My early experience in the National Cathedral in 1976, watching the wave pass through the congregation as row after row of worshippers bowed to the cross in procession, taught me the value of congregational participation in liturgy. In the years that followed, I experienced it as well in the practices of bowing or genuflecting when passing by the altar or crossing myself at certain times in the liturgy. These were personal acts of devotion that were shared with many around me.

As The Advocate was evolving, we sought ways to encourage congregational participation, and we embraced a practice of "participation over performance." Understanding that liturgy is meant to express and to form the people as the Body of Christ, wherever possible we encouraged active, not passive, participation. It took a while to stop some of the passive practices we inherited from our experiences in established churches, such as "passing the plate" at the offertory, and to engage in more participatory practices, such as an offertory procession of the whole congregation. Instead of a musical prelude, we adopted the "people's prelude" described earlier. We decided not to have a choir, but to sing together and to encourage everyone to sing wholeheartedly. Those particularly gifted with a voice for song were encouraged to come early on Sundays to learn the music, then to scatter throughout the congregation and lead the singing from there. We quickly became a singing congregation, embracing canons and *a cappella* opportunities.

A theologically trained woman in the congregation observed: "There is nothing that is more important than participation . . . Participation in life, participation in a community, participation in liturgy—it is the one and only way in which we experience the world outside of our own existence, to experience the other as part of our own humanity. Participation is how we know we are not entirely alone in the universe. This is not innate knowledge; this is only the kind of knowledge that can be obtained through action and experience."

Since we are a congregation with relatively few young children from eight to eighteen, everyone is encouraged to take a part in the roles usually given to young acolytes—crucifer, gospel bearer, and server. Some toddlers are visibly excited to be able to help their parent carry the cross. On occasion, we have two octogenarians serving together. Young adults who had never been to church, or not since they were children, experienced unexpected faith formation, lifting high the cross, holding the gospel book, and lighting the altar candles. An elder in a wheelchair lamented that she had nothing to offer, until someone realized she could hold the gospel in her lap and be pushed in procession by someone else.

Participation has also been fostered through the continued practice of sharing meals after the Eucharist every Sunday. We say that this meal is an "extension of the eucharistic feast," allowing us to "know more fully what it is to be the Body of Christ as we break bread together." Rather than a potluck, the meal is provided for all by a six-week rotation of dinner groups of four to six individuals who plan and cook the meals.

Such engaging, expressive, and formative involvement requires a lot of attention to scheduling with many people to sign up for one task or another. We regularly embrace the motto, "It takes a church to be the church!"

Questions for Reflection

1. How have you experienced participation in the liturgy?
2. What helps you to feel that you are part of the Body gathered?

There are other ways to start a church without a building, of course. Some new congregations rent a facility for their exclusive use, allowing for worship space, offices, and breakout rooms. This option is expensive, but it provides a location as well as the coveted visible sign, and certainly requires less energy to create a worship space every week. Other congregations choose a much simpler way, meeting in smaller groups in public venues without concern for any manifest expression of worship space. These missional gatherings take place in coffee shops, gyms, pubs, parks, and may or may not incorporate the Eucharist.

The Advocate was launched as a mission that would eventually become a self-sustaining parish of the Episcopal Church, with more than one hundred "adult confirmed communicants in good standing." And while we questioned some aspects of the tradition—who does what in the liturgy and why, what should be required for participation and membership in the church—we were also committed to the Book of Common Prayer declaration that the Holy Eucharist is "the principal act of Christian worship on the Lord's Day and other major Feasts." It was a given that we would include the Eucharist in our worship every Sunday and that a vested priest would preside.

Today the missionary impulse of the wider church in the world is pushing against the settings, the customs, the exclusionary barriers of some of our church's practices, especially the Eucharist. Who can receive? How do we invite? What are the essential elements? Not just bread and wine, but what about gluten free bread, a non-alcoholic alternative to the wine, particular words, physical presence, a priest's hands? These questions are causing the church to consider alternative ways of reaching and connecting with those who might not ever find their way into a church building or to a traditional eucharistic setting.

The Rev. Leslie Stewart, a former F16 fighter pilot and now a priest in Plano, Texas, leads a congregation of veterans and first responders in the "Warrior Church" that gathers in a gym. Many wear the "vestment" of a Warrior Church t-shirt, which creates a common identity and a community. The bell tolls, and they exercise their bodies, they tell and hear one another's stories, they encourage one another, and they celebrate the Eucharist. They belong. They are the Body of Christ. This ministry is rooted in the realization that there are many who would not be drawn to a traditional place and way of worship. There are many who have been wounded in body, mind, and soul, who yearn to connect with others and with God, and to be healed.

Some "missional expressions" meeting in restaurants punctuate the elements of an informal eucharistic rite with Bible study, conversation, and food. Others, meeting in pubs or homes without a priest or the Eucharist, are reaching out to new communities, neighborhoods, and demographics. Without the Eucharist and often led by laypersons, worship in secular settings can cast an even wider net to visitors. Often, these gatherings are launched and funded by established congregations of more traditional settings who are eager for the church to experiment with new expressions of church and with resources to share with the enterprise.

House Churches

House churches are emerging as an old/new model for church. The Rev. Audra Abt, missioner priest for a house church in Greensboro, North Carolina, has responded to the yearning of immigrant communities from Central and South America for house churches like those they belonged to in their countries of origin. These groups understand church primarily as the people of God, wherever they are gathered, with or without a priest. They meet to pray and reflect on the Word, studying the scriptures with an authority they know to be theirs as the Body of Christ. They trust that they will be given what they need to be church, and they trust the Spirit to have a hand in the teaching.

Given the constraints of work schedules, these groups usually gather on a Saturday evening. The priest attends once a month to offer the Eucharist and to connect them with the wider church. They may, on occasion, attend a service at *el templo* (the temple or church). But they are primarily lay led, and their identity as the Body of Christ is location specific, generally in their immediate neighborhood. Their mission is to be the Body of Christ in that place. They are to follow and serve Christ among their immediate neighbors. From the beginning, expression and formation is aligned with location.

It is common for every house to have a home altar, votive candles, and family practices of prayers and small offerings. When a home hosts a gathering of the church, its holy space is enlarged. Hospitality, inviting others into the home in the name of God, blesses the space. The people who come are part of consecrating a domestic place. With a liturgical sensibility, furniture is moved to make way for the gathering. The priest brings wine for the Misa/Mass, but invites the host to offer bread or a tortilla from their kitchen. This offering by the host also serves as a liturgical act.

The ministries of the people of the community emerge organically. Some have a gift of hospitality and host the gatherings. Some teach or provide pastoral care, encouraging others to share their stories and circumstances, discerning common concerns and thanksgivings, and weaving them into prayers.

Audra Abt suggests that for participants in a house church, the church is a community of the faithful aware that they are walking with Jesus and learning how they are called to be with God as they go. They gather where they live, among neighbors, in a shared context. When a crisis hits the neighborhood, the church is ready to help those in need. Members of the church community become the neighborhood organizers, doing so in the name of Jesus, aware of themselves as the Body of Christ, given for the world. Abt says that "One of the beautiful things about house church that I've learned is that the Body of Christ is the church in action in the world not just *wherever* we gather, but *whenever* we gather in Jesus's name."

Outdoor Church

Liturgies in outdoors settings, such as camps or conference centers, provide exceptional opportunities for the formation of the Body. Worshiping outdoors with a glorious view or around a campfire, inspired by a day of prayer and holy conversation or digging in the dirt to plant a garden, offers an experience of God as both immanent and transcendent. The intimacy of the retreat circle under the stars precludes any need for altar candles as a reminder of the holy. The wind would most likely blow them out anyway.

Camps and conference centers may have a care community, composed of some staff or nearby residents, but for the most part, the Body gathered at any given time is transient. How do these visitors know themselves to be part of a body when they have never worshiped together before and may never worship together again?

Such an extemporaneous gathering depends upon good liturgical leadership to create a worship experience of those gathered. A romantic liturgy around a campfire is not an end in itself. The congregation is being given an experience to carry home that may inspire the planning of future worship in small groups at home and in the larger gathered body at church. In these unconventional settings, the leader can encourage a shared vision among participants, in which they are together taking part in a life of faith and formation greater than a single parish or congregation, greater than the group here assembled. We might call this the BODY of Christ.

The BODY of Christ

The Great AMEN at the end of the eucharistic prayer is intentionally capitalized in bold letters to emphasize its significance. *Amen* means "I agree," I give my assent to what has been said. (The autocorrect on my smartphone once corrected "amen" to "I'm in." Well put!)

We might also use all capital letters to designate the distinction between our participation in the BODY of Christ—the One, Holy Catholic and Apostolic Church, the church throughout all ages, the Christ who was before time and will be forever—and the Body of Christ—the experience of the local congregation. Ideally, our experience of the Body gives us a glimpse of what it means to be part of the infinitely extensive BODY. This is especially true in liturgies and liturgical spaces that make us aware of the transcendence of God. A proper sense of the transcendent BODY cautions against particular pride in our singular local expression of the Body. It reminds us that we are not the sole expression of the BODY, whose continuity extends to other times and places. Being mindful of the experience of Christians in other hemispheres or our darker-skinned siblings, as discussed in chapter 3, can expand and strengthen our identity as part of the BODY of Christ.

However much we love our own congregation or denomination, or our branch of Christianity, Christ's BODY is more that any singular expression of the church. The truth cannot be contained. This can be as exciting as it is humbling. Along with leaders of retreats and conferences, we must all be mindful of the symbols and words that point us beyond the here, the now, the me, the us.

Formation of the Body Online

In the spring of 2020, I once again carried home the "stuff" of the church: processional cross, baptismal bowl, Paschal candle, stoles, the Tibetan bowl bell—the symbols and touchstones of our worship space, without the worship space itself. They were not in a trailer in the driveway this time, but in my dining room and den, serving as backdrops for our Sunday Zoom gatherings. Seventeen years of facing each other, singing together, breaking bread together, exchanging the Peace with one another, pridefully unplugged, our presence together in corporate worship had all come screeching to a halt, or so it seemed. The Covid-19 pandemic and subsequent stay-at-home practices gave us a whole new experience of church without a church building. How can we sing our holy song in a strange land, we wondered? How can we even sing?

My grandfather suffered a stroke the year I was born. It left him unable to speak or to swallow very well. He could not walk easily. The damage to his brain made him unable to write sentences or even words. Yet on Sunday mornings in my grandparents' kitchen, I remember my grandfather sitting in front of the television, watching the Mass broadcast from a Roman Catholic church. He was completely absorbed and focused. He was clearly gaining something from it. It was church.

I thought of my grandfather's experience when the worshiping church had to go online in 2020. Overnight, churches everywhere wrestled with the question: how are we going to do this?

Many churches chose livestreaming, inviting anyone to tune in and watch as a priest and several other clergy staff and/or lay leaders—standing six feet apart—performed the Sunday morning liturgy. Lessons, organ, homily, consecration, and communion remained unchanged. To many, there was comfort in the visible reassurance that, although disrupted, the life and rhythm of the church goes on. Those watching could also pray and sing along and be nourished.

Other churches livestreamed without the Eucharist, believing that a few should not share in the Eucharist until all could share it together. These churches either used the Liturgy of the Word from the eucharistic rite, ending with the Peace, or they used Morning Prayer. Some churches integrated pre-recorded pieces of the liturgy into the livestreamed liturgy. These were usually choir anthems or hymns, sermons or inspirational video clips. Others pre-recorded the entire liturgy.

Given The Advocate's particular emphasis on expression and formation of the Body in liturgy, there was never a question which platform we would use for our Sunday worship during the pandemic. Zoom allowed us to be live, engaging, and participatory. With everyone on Zoom, we could see one another, hear one another pray, proclaim, speak, and sing. The varying delays in sounds created a Pentecost/Babel effect that was at once irritating and energizing, as we could hear distinct voices within the chorus of voices. Unable to celebrate the Eucharist online together, we followed the liturgy of Morning Prayer, then later, the Liturgy of the Word, concluding with the Peace.

It took some weeks to work out the challenges. Previously shunned, PowerPoint was suddenly the means we needed. Our priest associate created a slide show that all could read looking at their screens while facing the camera, too. With each week's liturgy, we were better able to discern when we would unmute all and hear each other's voices in different tempos, and what parts of the service would best be read with only one voice unmuted, always with the reminder: "Each reader needs to unmute before reading." Now there's a rubric that Thomas Cranmer could never have imagined.

At first, we were painfully aware of what we were missing—the Eucharist, singing together, and seeing each other in person. Over time, though, as we moved from Lent to Holy Week to Eastertide, we found that the Prayers of the People were just as meaningful as they had always been, whether they offered aloud or in the chat box. And we quickly realized what we were gaining. Here was a way for us to be together when we weren't able to leave our homes. Moreover, each week, people from The Advocate diaspora—those who had moved to other parts of the country or world—were able to join us. It was like a homecoming. A woman who had recently moved to Iowa wrote: "It's been really meaningful to see all the different people of The Advocate from different times and in different places during this Covid time. It gives me a sense of being a part of something so much bigger but at the same time also very personal. I'm so thankful to get to experience some of that. I especially enjoy 'meeting' some of the people whose names I heard for many years but never got a chance to meet while there in person."

The previously distinct 9:00 a.m. and 11:00 a.m. congregations worshiped together, connecting anew. There was no crowded room to navigate or to limit contacts. In the minutes before the liturgy started, as each new face appeared in the gallery onscreen, cheers went up, greetings were offered, well-being queried, and visitors welcomed. At announcements time, proud parents introduced us to their newborns, a euphoric couple announced their engagement, and we sang to celebrate the ninety-sixth birthday of our beloved eldest elder. We could see each other smiling, clapping, waving, and singing. Poignantly, a woman who'd had a tumor removed on a Thursday was able to join us in worship on Sunday. "I hope my video is off!" she joked. Households with small children could "go to church" without the stress of having everyone dressed, fed, and into the car. Folks who would otherwise have joined us only on occasion were suddenly among the faces every Sunday.

But there were some who weren't there. Some who were unable or unwilling to worship digitally. Some found that the screen made them "swimmy headed." Others found it simply too painful to see people onscreen if they could not be with them. They said, "I'll be back when we are meeting in person again." Some had been drawn to The Advocate for our natural and unplugged vibe. They just didn't like tech church. In time, some dropped out with "Zoom fatigue."

Clergy and lay leadership committed to finding ways to hold us together, to allow everyone to remember who and whose they are. We created "virtual villages" and encouraged folks to meet for "virtual coffee," a one-to-one online. The vestry sent personal postcards out to everyone, and the clergy made a lot of phone calls. Over time, small groups started to meet safely by the pond on the church site. A desire for deeper connection led to the creation of "Advogroups," small groups meeting online or in person around a shared need or interest with prayer and mutual support. As diocesan and government restrictions eased, we held small, safe-distanced outdoor Eucharists, but remained clear that the Sunday morning "Advocate on Zoom" was the primary gathering of the body.

Online, it took a while to sort out how we could sing together. We knew that having everyone sing unmuted wouldn't work on the Zoom platform. We'd be on different notes, in different measures, at different times. It worked to have one person sing *a cappella* while everyone sang along from home, muted. About three months in, a member of the congregation emerged to be our "tech steward," organizing and producing videos of virtual choirs to lead us. Others recorded solo singing while playing guitar or piano. These diverse offerings engaged more people in our liturgical leadership, and helped to keep the liturgy fresh.

While we could not hear the entire congregation singing together, we could see each other singing. With the choirs and individuals leading us, a reminder that God loves to hear God's people sing, and encouragement to scan the Zoom gallery, the enthusiastic response was the robust singing in homes and on screened porches and decks across the region. It made us giddy.

Gradually we realized there was no longer anything "virtual" about our worship. It was real worship. We dropped "virtual" from our descriptions and drew a distinction between "online" worship and "in person" worship instead.

Was it liturgy? It was certainly the people gathered. Through it we expressed our faith in the Body of Christ, and we were being formed in our identity as the Body of Christ. It was not as public as could be, however. The potential threat of malicious hacking and disruption of Zoom gatherings ("Zoom bombing") precluded the public posting of the login site for our scheduled service gatherings. Visitors to our website could request access via email. After all those years of trying to lower the threshold of entry to make it as easy as possible for people to visit, now we needed to add additional steps into the church. Visitors had to persevere to log in, and while some did, we no doubt lost others. As Zoom developed its safeguards more fully with each passing month, we also became more confident in our Zoom abilities. We decided to take the risk of posting all Zoom logins on the website and on Facebook.

Congregations who chose the option of livestreaming clergy and a few others gathered in the church were more accessible to the public and experienced greater "traffic." Visitors who would likely have never gone into a church building were being fed by the liturgy and the faith, even if primarily by observing it and even if only in snippets. Recording the livestream and posting it online made it accessible to those who wanted to watch at different times of the day or week as well.

Other worshiping communities found ways to engage the congregation by more fully using pre-recorded video of new liturgical expressions. A golf cart procession, with households rolling by waving palms and shouting "Hosanna!" was filmed for Palm Sunday at St. Andrew's Episcopal Church in Boca Grande, Florida. For Grace Church in Waynesville, North Carolina, six households acted out six different Old Testament stories for the Liturgy of the Word for the Great Vigil of Easter, engaging children and their families in new and joyful ways and in a liturgy that is usually too late at night for them.

As with other expressions of church without a church building, online worship can shift the balance away from an awareness of the transcendence of God, God beyond us, and toward an awareness of the immanence of God, God among us. A video of the parish choir singing and organ playing, with images of vaulted ceilings and stained-glass windows, can have the unintended effect of making us wistful for—or lead us into the temptation of pride about—*our* particular architectural space, music program, or liturgy. Without the cues of the eucharistic gathering, we may too easily forget God in Christ beyond us. In the eucharistic gathering, we know the words we speak are words that have been spoken and the movements we make are movements that have been made by Christians gathered in their own particular time and place for millennia. In the eucharistic rite, we join our voices with angels and archangels and all the company of heaven as we lift our voices and sing, Holy, Holy, Holy Lord. . . .

In online worship, we are contained as either observers of the few who are engaging in the actions, or as a face in a box among other faces in boxes on a screen. In online worship, since there is a stronger tendency to reduce the rite to "these people, this screen," the presider must deliberately draw the body's attention to the rite's transcendent source and purpose, which enables them to see God beyond their own experience and place. This can be done by encouraging everyone to have a candle near at hand to light at the start of worship, or by letting the bell toll linger in the air and across the online connection. Introductions and reminders can also help.

When we recite the Nicene Creed and the Lord's Prayer in The Advocate's online worship, all are unmuted and are encouraged to imagine in the choral chaos the voices of Christians throughout the world and throughout the centuries, our spiritual ancestors, praying with us. The congregation is encouraged to slow the tempo, waiting at the end of each line for the delayed voices to catch up. This becomes a profound experience of Body awareness and formation, as all are attentive to one another, listening to one another. It takes more time to say the Lord's Prayer and the Creed this way. Reminded in liturgy that being attentive to others always takes more time, we are formed in patience.

Recording online liturgies makes them accessible at any time and to a wider public. Repeated viewing throughout the week provides comfort to many during the pandemic. Recorded church can create a temptation, however, to then view the liturgy as another form of entertainment, available on demand. In recorded liturgy the value of bodily presence is diminished, a presence that is of the essence of the God incarnate, God among us. Even so, we know that God is present in all things, and God can work through any medium. A pre-recorded absolution to confession is less than ideal, but it may give the viewer an experience of forgiveness nonetheless, and a hunger for more.

Question for Reflection

1. Have you had an experience of the Body of Christ or the BODY of Christ in online worship? What made it so?

One exciting development to emerge in the church's response to the pandemic is that it catalyzed new ways of thinking about church and liturgy. With props and traditional touchstones taken away, fruitful conversations began happening to enrich and to challenge our understanding of blessings, the Eucharist, worship, inclusion, the role of the priest, the presence of the people, and more. We became aware of what we missed and why, of what we were gaining, and what we could carry into the future. Without the Sunday Eucharist as the focal point of worship, our understanding expanded of the people gathered, faithful expression, and liturgy. For guidance and example, we looked to the church in regions with fewer clergy and more lay leaders who have provided worship and pastoral care between clergy visits for decades. We began to internalize what we may have said all along—that who we are and how we become the Body of Christ extends beyond the Sunday eucharistic liturgy and takes place beyond the church buildings.

Churches discovered ways of staying connected and engaged with one another apart from Sunday mornings. St. Dunstan's Episcopal Church in Madison, Wisconsin, created an entire video play about the story of their patron saint, St. Dunstan of Canterbury, with stay-at-home participation of many members of the congregation, as well as some pets. They then held a watch party for all to enjoy the production together. Other churches engaged in online Bible study or book studies. Food collections overflowed in the bell tower. A drive-by birthday celebration for a ten-year-old engaged dozens of parishioners in a liturgical celebration that would not have even occurred to the congregation pre-Covid-19.

For many during the pandemic, the end of the day was especially hard. People had trouble getting to sleep, especially if they had checked in on the news in the hours prior. The what ifs, the hows, and the realities of our personal lives, the community, and the nation were often alarming or discouraging. Those who live alone had no one with whom to process the day, the week, the season. Others looked for a peaceful transition from day to night just as much.

Prayer helps, and prayer in community with others can help even more. That is why The Advocate added Compline (nighttime prayers) on Zoom on Wednesdays at 8:30 p.m. The addition of Wednesday night Compline was simply to provide a way to gather and pray in the middle of the week, between the Sundays.

Very soon it became clear that this online Compline was more than that. It provided a welcome, needed way to end the evening in peace and in the company of others. It didn't require a significant time commitment, no more than fifteen minutes. It was calming to be with other human beings.

Within six weeks, Wednesday Compline became nightly Compline, each night led by a different lay person.

The Zoom link is posted on our website, and the link is the same every day, every week. Simple. The prayers are posted on the website too, so folks can download them for their own prayer time or use them to follow along on the Zoom. We use the Book of Common Prayer rite, with psalms and prayers and the *Nunc Dimittis*, and also a time of intercessory prayer. That rite is supplemented by the closing prayer and benediction of the Night Prayer from *A New Zealand Prayer Book*. This ending washes over and through those gathered like a gentle blessing and a holy sedative. Each element is part of the economy of it all—the ancient, the time transcending, the present, the personal, the communal.

A steady core is on the Compline Zoom each night, and others join as they are able. The regulars came from four different counties. Those with small children join if the kids were in bed on time. Sometimes they invite their older children to participate.

Each night, when the liturgy concludes, those gathered happily and sleepily bid one another good night.

After several attempts to add the daily office to The Advocate's liturgical offerings through the years, both in person and online,

Covid gave us the inclination and the desire to make it happen. Zoom made it possible. Compline provided us the essential content and doable duration.

Realizing that people were missing "communion" and not just the Eucharist, about ten folks of The Advocate got together (safely) and crafted small bowl-shaped cups, one for every household of The Advocate, all from a single block of clay. A glazed and fired cup was distributed to each household, including those in the diaspora. The cups were then used in a brief "Liturgy of Longing," adapted from an essay by Br. James Koester of the SSJE, for use in the season of Advent 2020. The act of using the roughly hewn Advocate cup became a means of connection and an experience of communion with the church.

Questions for Reflection

1. Did you discover something new in worshiping online in 2020? What was it?

2. How can online worship best engage the congregation?

3. How can online worship best welcome the stranger?

4. What advantages and disadvantages of liturgy in a church building have you realized?

5. What practices, if any, from 2020 do you hope to continue into the future?

The Angelus Revisited

It is not uncommon for Episcopal communities to provide a regular gathering for Morning Prayer or Evening Prayer during the week. These peaceful rites are an important and formative part of our Anglican tradition that some would even say is central. The rites provide an anchor in the midst of weekday busyness, a comfort and blessing even for those church members who aren't able to visit there every day. Increasingly, especially in urban and suburban churches, membership is scattered far and wide during the week. And in Covid time, gatherings in person are limited, even impossible.

Gathering online is one solution. The old custom of the Roman Catholic Church of praying the *Angelus* offers another. This custom is perhaps best known by the painting with that name by the nineteenth-century French painter Jean-François Millet. People scattered hither and yon would hear the church bells toll at particular times of the day—morning, noon, and evening. They would stop what they were doing and offer a prayer of thanksgiving for the Incarnation and of petition for God's grace. Very formative, and very public.

A modern-day *Angelus* is made possible by the gadgets we carry. Clocks of smartphones and computers can be set to give an alarm or reminder at different times of the day. Those willing can agree that at a certain time, wherever they are, they will offer a prayer. Not the entirety of a daily office, but at least a psalm or canticle agreed upon each month, or even a simple thanksgiving to God. They offer their prayer at the given time, knowing that others of the congregation were praying at the same time. Together they pray. Together they are formed.

Each participant comes to know that they are part of something intimate and also part of something bigger than themselves. Others with them, wherever they are in that hour, learn that they are connected to the church as they explain why their phone is sounding. It becomes a small public witness, even as it is a personal practice.[16]

5 | The Life of a Church as Meta-Liturgy

In late 2012, the Episcopal Church of the Advocate moved a church building. An 1891 Carpenter Gothic Episcopal church building, long out of public use, was hauled across one hundred thirty miles of back roads of the North Carolina piedmont from its original home, a few miles north of Winston-Salem, to its new home in Chapel Hill. There, we added insulation, electricity, and plumbing. From beginning to end, it was a liturgical experience.

I have said that the Sunday eucharistic liturgy is an experience of primary formation of the Body of Christ. I have also said that this formation takes place by means of other special occasions for liturgy in a variety of settings. I want to suggest that even acts and events not formally identified as liturgy can be considered liturgical, and that the entire life of a church can be viewed as a kind of meta-liturgy.

Every Sunday at The Advocate, we remind ourselves that the liturgy is, among other things, the work of the people. Liturgy is what we do together. Over time, the congregation began to consider all the things we do together as a community to be the "work of the people"—site stewardship, pledge drives, Sunday lunches, serving meals at the homeless shelter, and more. It slowly dawned on me that each of these activities can be considered liturgical events. They are both the work of the people and a public work, expressing what we believe and forming who we become. Two particular events in the history of The Advocate clarify this.

Because we are a relatively new Episcopal congregation, The Advocate community is more or less aware of the details of our history. But with new people joining year by year, it is a challenge to keep our history alive. Regardless of how long they have been a part of The Advocate, there are two events in particular that all people of the church know about. These original events, and the subsequent telling of them, express what we believe; they have formed who we have become as the Body of Christ. The first of these two expressive and formational events was the move of the church building.

The Advocate Chapel

St. Philip's Episcopal Church, which was built for the Episcopalians of Germanton, North Carolina, in 1891, could seat 150 people. The congregation peaked in 1895 with twenty-two members, then local people were drawn to the growth and expansion of the Episcopal church in nearby Winston-Salem. The occasional services of a priest and about ten faithful folks in any given decade kept the church going for the next eight-five years, but by 1980, the building had become an "historic property" of the diocese. For thirty years after that, volunteers gathered twice a year to tend to the property and hold a service of thanksgiving. In 2010, with no volunteers left to carry on the tradition, the building was closed and left untended.

The following year, The Advocate, having purchased land, had begun planning to raise funds to build a small chapel. A member of the diocesan historic properties commission approached us and asked if we might consider moving the St. Philip's church building from Germanton to Chapel Hill. Consider it we did. Our adventure began.

The move first required dismantling the bell tower and the roof, board by board, to clear the power lines along the one hundred thirty miles of central North Carolina our chapel would travel. Restoration specialists removed the stained-glass windows for safekeeping. As each window was gently pulled from its casement, rot and decay appeared among the field mice nests and nineteenth-century straw insulation. The handmade bricks of the foundation pillars, which had held the building up off the ground for over a century, were too crumbled for re-use and were discarded. Throughout the several weeks of deconstruction, brick by board by stained-glass window, people from The Advocate drove to Germanton to witness the activity and to take photos to share with folks back home.

A metaphor of new life for an old church began to unfold. Where possible, we worked to preserve the functional integrity and aesthetic beauty inherent to the building. Some parts didn't need preservation; they needed restoration or rebuilding. Other parts had to be left behind.

Using a large crane, the movers eased the bell tower onto a flatbed. What remained of the roofless structure was given an interior skeleton and shrink-wrapped for weatherproofing and stability. With state-of-the-art jacks and other equipment, the old church was loaded onto a large truck for transport. Such an oversized load could not be moved along the interstate, but only on back roads. Every mile of the route was planned and approved by local jurisdictions; road closures and police escorts were arranged. The metaphor expanded: moving a church, like liturgy, takes time, care and thought, preparation, and collaboration.

On moving day, folks from The Advocate and residents of Germanton gathered at the church site for prayers. The pastor and people of the Germanton Baptist Church next door participated. The Rev. Canon Marilyn McCord Adams, then a priest associate at The Advocate, wrote the following prayer for the occasion:

> O God, you have never been one to settle down. You are always on the move, calling us to be fellow travelers, ready and willing—like Abraham—to leave home for places we have never been before. O God, bless St. Philip's Church on its journey from Germanton that built it, to Chapel Hill that prepares to welcome it. Protect its fabric. Support the drivers who edge its parts down rural roads and village streets. Make skilled workers nimble to put it back together again. Keep blowing through it with the wind of your spirit. No matter who enters, set their hearts on fire.

We sang "Amazing Grace."

The palpable excitement of a great journey beginning was like a hot air balloon lifting off or a steam locomotive rolling across the countryside. We all held our breath as truck and building moved slowly—very slowly—onto the road. The men who worked to keep the load level and steady slipped about the precious cargo, keeping an eye on every corner and side, studying monitors, tires, and springs. Onto the main street, branches cleared above, the building moved ahead.

A teenager of The Advocate loaned us her cell phone (an amazing sacrifice!) so that we had a GPS signal on the truck to track its location day by day, even hour by hour. People could link to the signal from The Advocate's webpage and monitor the progress through the weeks that followed. Advocates drove over from Chapel Hill as they were able, to meet up with the church building on its route, pulling over by a sugar cane or tobacco field to wait for the entourage to pass. First came the police escorts in cars or motorcycles, then the building itself. The truck driver honked and waved. It was happening. We were filled with a spirit of anticipation, vitality, and progress. Four days, six days, ten days, a dozen. At night the old church slept in the parking lots of wayside general stores or businesses. Reports started coming in from around the diocese: "We saw your church by the side of the road."

Meanwhile, back in Orange County, the work crews and people of The Advocate were readying the building's new site. We gathered on a winter evening. Lamps removed from the historic building were lit to mark the site in the shape of a cross. We sang, we prayed, we rang the old church bell. Fundraisers were organized to help with the costs of moving and restoring the chapel. Members of the congregation created concerts, a silent auction, a quilt raffle, and yard sales. And, of course, we made a t-shirt sporting the slogan "Church on the Move." Everybody was involved in one way or another.

The night before the building rolled onto its new location in north Chapel Hill, it rested by the side of the road near Hillsborough, which is just north of the town. A group from The Advocate went to its berth there and prayed evening prayers. As cars blew by, we celebrated the church on the move and realized that we were being formed for our future in ways we did not yet know.

The day of delivery was festive and bright, as balloons and streamers waved in the breeze. We were full of excitement for what we had done and for the future ahead.

The truck arrived early. People ran from their cars parked along the traffic-blocked road. Children took turns ringing the old bell that was temporarily removed from the bell tower and placed on the old well-top near the site. We removed the original pulpit from the church, and we offered prayers of thanksgiving. Then we had cake.

St. Philip's Church began its new life as The Advocate Chapel.

As that first exhilarating hour faded and the day wore on, our focus turned to anticlimactic practical matters such as adjustments of the building to the site, with temporary foundation and braces, building the new brick foundation pillars, and getting the roof back on.

There was a lot of mud.

So began another sixteen months of repairing, building, decision making, and waiting. Change comes slowly to the church. But if the Holy Spirit is alive and stirring, change is going to come. The call of the faithful is to be on the lookout for that movement of the Spirit, and to be ready to respond.

The move of the chapel was a liturgical event, public and corporate.[17] It reflected our belief in a God who moves in and through the church. It gave us a profound experience of stewardship. We knew that we were not now owners of the chapel; we were now stewards of a building built for God's people for another season of its life, to serve God's people in this season. That awareness of stewardship rather than ownership called us to be generous in sharing the building with others.

The move also confirmed for us twenty-first-century Christians that we are rooted in customs and practices far older than we are. We value and cherish those old ways, yet we do not need to be bound by them. We can make some new, we can restore or repurpose others, and some will need to be discarded.

The move expressed for us our communal and inclusive nature, as well as our desire to mix the old and the new, the expected and the serendipitous. Most profoundly, the move expressed the faith of the people of The Advocate as the Body of Christ, and it helped to form us as the Body of Christ. Framing the adventure this way helped us to make it through the next sixteen months of renovation and construction and has sustained us through the ensuing years.

The move of the chapel was powerfully symbolic, meaningful, and formational in the life of The Advocate. However, after we settled into the building, we realized that practically overnight we had become "the cute little church" on Homestead Road. That image soon challenged other fundamental characteristics of our faith community. Thankfully, a timely second event provided a new catalyst for forming and informing the people of The Advocate—the development of the Pee Wee Homes.

The Pee Wee Homes

Pee Wee Homes is a collaborative effort to allow those with a history of chronic homelessness to live in beautiful, affordable, free-standing tiny homes. Over a period of three years, a handful of professionals—a few from The Advocate, and more from the wider community—gathered to craft one part of a solution to the affordable housing crisis in our town. Architects, lawyers, social workers, builders, staff from the Self Help Credit Union, and staff from a local non-profit familiar with the needs of the homeless met to develop a model for beautiful affordable rental homes for people in our area whose income is less than thirty percent of the average median income. We wanted to build three of these homes, each less than 350 square feet, on The Advocate site, with the hope of inspiring other churches to consider doing the same. We worked our way through town requirements, state requirements, and diocesan requirements. A significant amount of the funding came from Chapel Hill's newly created affordable housing fund. Local foundations supported the project as well, and a good deal of fundraising was done by students at the University of North Carolina. To build the houses, we collaborated with Habitat for Humanity, which coordinated volunteers from the town, the university, the wider community, and the church. Building this way took time, but the collaboration helped us cut costs and gave more people the opportunity to be a part of it all.

Now The Advocate leases the homes to the newly formed Pee Wee Homes non-profit. Three men, who had been homeless for a decade or more, each live in their own home on The Advocate site. The men pay a modest, affordable rent to Pee Wee Homes. The people of The Advocate are joyful and proud to be part of a church that hosts these men in the three tiny houses.

Taking place over three years, the Pee Wee Homes project provided ample opportunity for the clergy and people of The Advocate to reflect on our commitment to share what resources we have—in this case land—with the community around us. This formed us in our response to meeting the needs of the poor, and in our call to work collaboratively with others, within and outside of the church. Importantly, this experience also formed us to seek other opportunities for collaboration in the future.

Every church has events in its past or practices in its present that give the church a particular identity in the public eye. Some events were very much the work of the people, and some were very much a public work, made more public by media coverage. These public works that express and shape the faith and identity of the congregation are liturgical expressions of the church.

Liturgical expressions of the church might also include events of a particular day or season—the seven months when the congregation rallied to provide companionship for an ailing elder, the day the bonfire got out of control and everyone had to help put it out before it spread any further, the Lent when everyone did an energy audit of their homes and gave up excess wattage for a season, or the month when the final payment was made on the church building loan.

In addition to single events, there are other, ongoing public works in our churches—food pantries, coffee shops, preschools, meals for the sick, and day care programs. But too often, when we think of our church's history and identity, we focus on the clergy in charge or the construction of buildings. At The Advocate, our shared meals Sunday by Sunday are significant events, on a par with any priest or building, forming us to be the Body of Christ.

The Meta-Liturgy

Realizing so many events that could be considered liturgical in the life of a church beyond the Sunday liturgy, it becomes apparent that the whole scope of a church's life can be viewed as a meta-liturgy. Not only the Sunday gatherings or various occasions throughout a given year or a given lifetime, our understanding of liturgy can be expanded to mean the whole of our public life together as church: the stewardship of our land and buildings—how they are used and shared, or not—what appears in our operating budget, how we engage with the community around us, our practice of hospitality. The entire story of a particular congregation through the years reflects this meta-liturgy. The story we inherit and the story we create expresses who we are and shapes us for our life in the world. The more we are aware of and intentional about this expression and formation, the more robustly we can become the Body of Christ that we receive in the eucharistic liturgy.

I do not intend for the expansion of the word liturgy to take away from the primacy of the term with regards to the Sunday Eucharist. The Sunday eucharistic liturgy is the point of focus, the primary place for our expression and formation as the Body of Christ. It is in that liturgy that we are given the foundation, the framework, the core of all that we believe and all that we are. If we are able to expand our definition and our understanding of liturgy, however, to include all of our public work as church, opportunities for our formation as the Body of Christ will increase as well. Strengthened in our identity, we will more ably serve a world so desperately in need of God's love.

In chapter 2, I suggested that the moment we walk through the doors of a church on a Sunday morning, we can learn a lot about what a particular congregation values or believes. From the start, we gain a sense of what is important in that congregation's faith and practice, how it holds the balance between the immanence and transcendence of God, the cultivation of personal and corporate faith, and the value of "perfection" and "come as you are."

Similarly, a church's meta-liturgy often begins in the conception and early years of a church's life. The vision for the church, the circumstances under which it was launched, and events of its early years can be templates for patterns that shape the congregation's identity for decades. Sometimes this is called a church's "DNA." But to call it the DNA makes it feel inescapable or locked in. If we see our early life as part of our liturgy, we can glean from it those things that continue to express and form us today. And if what we see doesn't form us more fully as the Body of Christ, then, like the crumbling bricks of the early foundation of The Advocate Chapel, they can be left behind.

The Advocate was born of the generous collaboration of our diocese and the three established parishes in our county. It is understandable, then, that we would lean into collaboration with others in the community for the development of the Pee Wee Homes. The success of that project makes us more likely to enter into collaborative efforts in the future. Collaboration will likely continue to be part of our church's meta-liturgy.

The fact that we were born of the generous risk-taking of others leads us to be generous with new ministries in our midst, and to take risks without assurance that a particular ministry will flourish. Further, our sponsoring parishes modeled support without meddling or directing. That has become a model we inherit and embrace. Some ministries take root and bloom perennially the way they were first envisioned. Others are like "annuals," with a short but vibrant life. Some ministries change from one season to the next as different people assume leadership.

For a season, The Advocate office was located on a busy street in town that featured a ramp and wooden deck. That year we had a tea-and-conversation-loving intern who hosted "Theology on Deck." We advertised "tea will be served." This was very public and engaged drop-ins from town as well as people of The Advocate. The effort floundered, however, under the regular attendance of antagonistic anti-Christian visitors. The project went on hiatus for a few years, and then reemerged as "Theology on Tap" led by a lay theologian of The Advocate. Held in a local brewery for over two years, this effort thrived as "Indulgences: formerly Theology on Tap" (due to a copyright conflict). When the facilitator moved on to become the Episcopal chaplain at Duke University, Indulgences ended, perhaps to emerge again in another form in the future.

Other ministries evolve. Our Sunday "extension of the eucharistic feast" started out as simple savory snacks to tide us over for the Christian education time that followed. As we came to appreciate the expressive and formational aspects of the gathering around food, we moved from shared snacks to a shared meal, and we found other ways to provide Christian education for a season. Soon, we found ways to create a Sunday schedule that allowed for equal emphasis on the ministry of the shared meal and the ministry of Christian education.

Then came a lay volunteer who wanted to bring people together over a meal in The Advocate's House on a weeknight, too. Wednesday night "house dinners" emerged, with another shared meal along with equal parts open fellowship and focused conversations. The focus was provided by a prompt such as an experience of shelter, a description of a mentor, something you want to leave behind in your life, something you want to cultivate in your life, an experience as a sibling or as a single child, and so forth. These prompts brought focus and self-revelation into the mix. A candle was passed, and people were invited one at a time to respond to the prompt for a few minutes. It was a time for sharing and for listening, not for conversation. Connections among those gathered deepened and a practice of mutual care and good food developed that extended beyond those gathered, beyond Wednesday nights, and into other aspects of our community life.

When Covid hit in 2020, Wednesday night house dinners became "House Dinner without Dinner." The gathering, the prompts, and the deep fellowship continued on Zoom. Those who gathered were grateful and also looked forward to the day that dinner would return, honoring The Advocate practice of gathering around food and breaking bread together.

From the beginning, The Advocate has also valued inclusion. It started with our launch in the season after the vote in the General Convention of the Episcopal Church in 2003 to approve the election and consecration of the partnered gay priest Gene Robinson, opening the way for him to become bishop of the Diocese of New Hampshire. It was clear to us from the start that The Advocate would be inclusive and supportive of the LGBTQ community. We received this as a call to lead with inclusion, whether in terms of sexual orientation, ability, economic means, age, or stage of life.

Another thread that runs through our meta-liturgy is a willingness, even an enthusiasm, to embrace change. The Advocate was launched in part to be a twenty-first-century expression of the Episcopal/Anglican tradition. We have worshipped in three different locations in our first fifteen years, with offices in four different locations. We change the liturgy from season to season. We try something new almost every season. Sometimes it works and we bring it back again the following year, sometimes it does not work and we let it go. Someone came to us with a chanted Nicene Creed that they learned on retreat in a monastery. We tried it for a season, and it stuck. It became a staple of our Sunday worship together. For us, singing the Creed engages our hearts in love of God. Another year, for the season of Epiphany we tried a spiral processional. That did not work.

Our unofficial motto is "Nothing is set in stone, except the love of God." This prepared us well for the changes that came our way in 2020 with the Covid-19 virus, heart-hurting though some of those changes were.

Collaboration, generosity of spirit, inclusion, change—these were all part of The Advocate's entrance rite and are the hallmarks of the meta-liturgy of The Advocate today.

The meta-liturgy is also shaped by a church's scandals and divisions. An affair by priest, an embezzlement by a treasurer, or a mishandled firing of a staff member are some things that can tarnish and haunt a community for decades. The church is never immune to the sins of the people within it. Clergy and laity alike are all sinful, broken human beings. Whether we are at church or in the world, what we do and what we say has the power to weave the fabric of the community or to tear it; to build up the body or to hinder it. The tearing and hindering is often caused by abuse of power or of trust, usually with sex or money. How we respond as church can express and form our identity as the Body of Christ. As the Body of Christ, we are called to pray for the offender as well as the offended; we strive for forgiveness, and also for justice; we listen to one another and we pray for one another.

Six years into our young life, The Advocate was rocked by the unexpected and widely publicized arrest of a member of our community. He was a leading layperson at The Advocate, serving on the vestry and facilitating our anti-racism work. But in his private life he was trespassing on the body and soul of a small boy. His arrest hit us hard, and we responded with disbelief, sorrow, anger, and fear. We came together as church, heard the facts, heard one another's pain, concerns, and memories, and we prayed. A few days later, we did it again. And when we gathered for Sunday's liturgy, we heard the words of the Collect for Purity more profoundly than ever:

"Almighty God, to you all hearts are open, all desires known, and from you no secrets are hid. . . ."

In the season that followed, we held the victims of his trespass in prayer, remembering them each time the Prayers of the People invited us to intercede for those who suffer, for those in any need or trouble. We also prayed for him, by name, as one in prison. This was not easy. Some found it impossible, unconscionable that we would pray for someone who had abused a child, for someone who had betrayed the community. Some quit the prayers, some quit the church. More pain.

But those who persevered were formed as a people who know the brokenness of our lives and of our world, who pray for those who hurt us, who do not shy from justice, who come together in times of sorrow and hurt. We each realized more fully our own complexities and our own need for forgiveness. We felt the presence of the One who knows the sufferings and injustices of life. We came to understand more fully our need for Christ's Body, broken for us, and what it means to be formed as Christ's Body wounded, and given for the world.

This too was liturgical.

Questions for Reflection

1. Was there a time when the fabric of your church community was torn?
2. Was it mended? If so, how?
3. How is that event described, or not, today?
4. Should it be?

The Body of Christ is given for the world. We are not the only ones who behold what we are. The world beholds us as well. Our life and work shape the image of the Body of Christ in the wider community. In all that we are and all that we do, the church gives witness to the loving, liberating, life-giving God, or fails to.

Some are formed by belonging to a church known for welcoming children with special needs, or to a church that is known for its beautiful stained-glass windows or for its choral music program. Some are part of a church known for ministry to and with the poor in the heart of the city, while others are part of a church in the affluent suburbs known for the annual blessing of the backpacks.

Because of our commitment to inclusion in 2003, The Advocate quickly became known as a "gay-friendly church." Within our first two years, we also developed relationships with a prisoner on death row and with a local community of chronic and severely mentally ill adults. We gained a reputation for justice work and social ministry. And because our bishop gave us relatively loose reins for our liturgical prayers and practices, we were able to develop a lively, engaging, participatory liturgy, clearly rooted in the tradition, but with twenty-first-century sensitivities to hospitality and diversity. The Pee Wee Homes brought The Advocate newspaper and television coverage, which translated into a reputation for providing affordable housing.

The Advocate's identity in the wider community and the church has shifted over time. We no longer stand out among churches that have become more inclusive of the LGBTQ community. We no longer have an organized ministry with mentally ill adults, although mentally ill adults know that they are welcomed in our life. We continue to find ways to live and work for justice and offer social ministry, such as the Pee Wee Homes, and to carry on the work of racial reconciliation. What seemed exceptional in the mid-aughts—5:00 p.m. worship on Sundays, no bulletins, no formal committees other than the vestry, and so forth—has now become less so as the wider church has become more experimental and creative. We find ourselves in a middle way between established churches and more contemporary missional expressions. But we are still known for our engaging liturgy and our creative problem solving, and for a wisdom and authenticity we know has been born of our pain.

Our life beyond worship becomes liturgical as we are able to answer these questions and when we can remind ourselves of the answers as we experience an event or describe a ministry. Our life as church becomes a meta-liturgy as we become ever more aware of the way in which our embodied actions express our faith and form our identity as the Body of Christ.

My hope is that in the years to come, the move of The Advocate Chapel is remembered not only as an exciting, quirky event, but also as a foundational action that continues to express and form our faith. My hope is that formed in the knowledge of our history, we can know creative, collaborative, or even risky endeavors may take a little longer, will be more challenging than easy, will require perseverance, and yet will also make a profound difference in the formation and faith of individuals and of the body.

This will happen if we live into our story and remind ourselves of it. "That's when we moved the chapel" becomes "When we moved the chapel, we expressed our commitment to conserve resources and to honor the past and make it new." It will happen in other congregations when "That's when we built the building" becomes "That's when we built the facility that allowed us to better serve the poor, or to engage with community around us, or to welcome the stranger." Maybe add, "It reminds us that God comes into the world in Christ, and we who are the Body of Christ are to make that known."

It may be a mouthful. But people get used to it. The Rev. William Barber has made it clear that the Poor People's Campaign isn't just the Poor People's Campaign. No. It is "The Poor People's Campaign: A National Call for Moral Revival." That's a mouthful. But every bit of it counts.

As church people, we may live in hope and expectation that others will find our liturgy meaningful simply by being there, with further instructions unnecessary. John Westerhoff, my liturgics professor at Duke, repeated the adage over and again: "It's easier to act ourselves into a new way of thinking than it is to think ourselves into a new way of acting."

This is a good basic teaching for liturgy; through it, over time, we indeed act ourselves into a new way of thinking and of being. But as noted in chapter 1, the church can no longer expect the participation that allows for such formation over time. We may need to jumpstart the new way of thinking and being that the liturgy provides by intentionally adding educative and formational phrasing here and there, and encouraging others to do the same. This is true Sunday by Sunday, and in the whole life of the church.

Building the Pee Wee Homes on The Advocate campus was a liturgical event that will form the people of The Advocate more deeply when we are able to say, "The Pee Wee Homes are homes for those who would otherwise be homeless. We are hosting them in response to our call as Christians to serve the poor and to respect the dignity of every human being."

Words matter in liturgy. Yes they do. And they matter in our formation as church, the Body of Christ.

1. How would you craft a timeline for the celebration of your church's milestone anniversary—a fifth, tenth, twenty-fifth, or one hundredth? What is important to include?

2. In what way do you associate particular liturgies, clergy, staff, or buildings with your understanding of what it means for your church to be the Body of Christ?

Looking Forward—Interdigitation

In the mid-twentieth century, households across America were taken up in the excitement of new gadgetry and materials. Instant coffee simplified morning routines. Electric can openers and electric knives appeared under the Christmas tree. Wall-to-wall acrylic carpet and vinyl covered the old hardwood floors. It took some decades for us to realize that that sharp kitchen knives from the back of the drawer worked just as well or better, that wall-to-wall acrylic carpet works well in some rooms but not in every room, that instant coffee has its place in our life, but it may not be best every day.

Like the Church of the Advocate, born in the early years of the twenty-first century, the church across the land is being challenged to discern anew the parts of the church that should be preserved or restored, what can be discarded, and what needs to be created from scratch. Put another way, "things which were cast down are being raised up, and things which had grown old are being made new" (BCP, 528).

In Covid time we are discovering ways that the internet can bring us together. After the Covid crisis passes, the church will need to take time to find ways to use the internet effectively, to strengthen the Body rather than fracture it. The words of one Advocate ring in my ears: "I'm going to be sixty-seven years old next month. I don't want to have to only experience church online simply because I'm in a high-risk group (over sixty-five), while all the young people and children get to gather in the chapel."

Setting up a camera in the nave for livestreaming will lower the threshold for entry for the curious. But it will not be sufficient for the Body. We will need to be creative in order to create and sustain forms of online worship that (as much as possible) are equally attractive, equally engaging to our in-person worship.

As we continue to dwell in a world of digital as well as physical viruses, the church will need to reconsider the particulars of how we gather, how we identify ourselves as a community, even how we celebrate the Eucharist. We will need to continue to debate what words will form our common prayer and what words will allow the Gospel to be understood by diverse people. Audra Abt in the house church reminds me that continually referring to church on "Sunday" marginalizes those who have to work on Sunday and find church on another day of the week. Similarly, our beloved nineteenth-century Anglican hymnody will continue to enfold some in worship while keeping others away.

In a Zoom meeting of a diocesan task force created to discern how we would move forward from the stay-at-home season of Covid-19, a doctor priest introduced the term "interdigitation." It refers to the interlacing of the fingers, as if in prayer. For the purposes of the church looking forward, this means the integration of practices. We won't have the old without the new, we won't have the new without the old. All will be folded in together.

I like this concept because it is reminiscent of the old children's rhyme, "Here's the church, here's the steeple, open the door, where are the people?" First the rhyme is told with the fingers folded on the outside so that the church created by the folded hands appears empty. Then the hands are folded a different way, with the fingers interlaced underneath. Where are the people? There they are! I want to use the rhyme now, to emphasize the concept of interdigitation and to show that the people are not only in the building. Indeed, the building may be empty sometimes, but the church is flourishing.

I also like the concept of interdigitation because it is physical, of the Body, and brings us back to Paul and his metaphor way back when:

> For as in one body we have many members, and not all the members have the same function, so we, who are many, are one body in Christ, and individually we are members one of another. (Romans 12:4–5)

> [S]peaking the truth in love, we must grow up in every way into him who is the head, into Christ, from whom the whole body, joined and knit together by every ligament with which it is equipped, as each part is working properly, promotes the Body's growth in building itself up in love. (Ephesians 4:15–16)

When the move to online worship was necessitated by the pandemic in 2020, the church's liturgical reflection and preparation broadened. We had to consider anew how to be public and how to be in the world while also tending to the body of those we already know and love. We realized that when taken outside of a church building, our liturgical imagination expands. We start to see opportunities for the public expression and formation of the Body of Christ, given for the world, in all we do together.

The challenge before us is to resist the collective penchant to "go back" to the way we did church before the pandemic. Instead we need to move forward into the future, integrating what we have experienced and learned in the time of Covid. We need to keep asking the questions that have been thrust upon us. What is essential in worship, in sacrament, and in roles of the ordained and the laity? What is the threshold for entry and what does entry mean? How do we gather? How do we exchange the Peace? How do we partake of the eucharistic sacrament? What is the purpose of our worship together? What is our liturgy? Is it public? How does it express what we believe and form what we become? How do we be and become the Body of Christ? A season of church without a church building has propelled us into the twenty-first century. The Holy Spirit has once again proven herself to be alive and well and moving within us and among us and beyond us. How will we respond?

Behold what you are: the Body of Christ, given for the world. So many members, individuals who make up congregations, congregations that make up denominations or regions or eras, denominations or regions or eras that make up the Church Universal. United in baptism, called to know and make known the loving, liberating, life-giving Way of God. May we become what we receive, in the bread that is blessed, in the liturgy of the church that forms us.[18]

Questions for Reflection

1. Have you had an experience of "interdigitation" in the church? Was it expansive or disjointed? What made it so?

2. Can you imagine ways to interdigitate (now, there is a word!) the internet and in-person gatherings in the seasons ahead that will strengthen the Body of Christ?

Notes

1 A fabulous description of the shopping mall as cathedral is given in James K. A. Smith, *Desiring the Kingdom: Worship, Worldview, and Cultural Formation* (Grand Rapids, MI: Baker Academic, 2009), 19–22.

2 Karen Hutzel and Susan Cerulean, "Taking Art Education to the Streets: 'The Procession of the Species' as Community Arts," *Journal of Cultural Research in Art Education* 21 (2003): 36–43.

3 The Episcopal Church, "Liturgy," *An Episcopal Dictionary of the Church*, https://episcopalchurch.org/library/glossary/liturgy.

4 This is a descriptive expression used by the Most Rev. Michael Curry, presiding bishop of the Episcopal Church.

5 Alexander Schmemann, *For the Life of the World: Sacraments and Orthodoxy* (Yonkers, NY: St. Vladimir's Seminary Press, 1973), 27.

6 Samuel Wells, *Crafting Prayers for Public Worship: The Art of Intercession* (Norwich: Canterbury Press, 2013), 41.

7 Goffredo Boselli, *The Spiritual Meaning of the Liturgy: School of Prayer, Source of Life* (Collegeville, MN: Liturgical Press, 2014), 121–23.

8 Ann Quito, "What Choral Singing Can Teach Us about Leadership," *Quartz at Work*, December 12, 2018, https://qz.com/work/1491154/what-chorale-singing-can-teach-us-about-leadership/.

9 Augustine, *Confessions*, trans. R.S. Pine-Coffin (London: Penguin Books, 1961), 238–39.

10 https://www.merriam-webster.com/dictionary/dismiss.

11 The Rev. Jamonde Taylor of St. Ambrose Episcopal Church in Raleigh, North Carolina, presented insights about light and darkness and race, the January 2020 Rooted in Jesus Conference in Atlanta, "Wrapped in Whiteness: Worship, Liturgy and Race," and at the October 2020 webinar of the Episcopal Church Standing Commission on Liturgy and Music, "A Gathering on Liturgical Formation."

12 Reports of the Committees, Commissions, Agencies and Boards of The General Convention of the Episcopal Church, Seventy-Fourth General Convention, Minneapolis, Minnesota, July 30–August 8, 2003 (New York: Church Publishing, 2003), 170.

13 "Egeria's Description of the Liturgical Year in Jerusalem: Translation, Based on the Translation Reproduced in Louis Duchesme's Christian Worship (London, 1923)," *Egeria and the Fourth Century Liturgy of Jerusalem*, hypertext version by Michael Fraser, University of Durham, 1994, http://users.ox.ac.uk/~mikef/durham/egetra.html.

14 Dennis G. Michno, "A Form for Blessing Holy Water," in *A Priest's Handbook: The Ceremonies of the Church* (Harrisburg, PA: Morehouse Publishing, 1983), 266.

15 Note: Some parts of the chapter were originally published on the Episcopal Church Vital Practices blog.

16 An earlier version of this story appeared on Episcopal Café, April 2013, https://www.episcopalcafe.com/memorization_and_formation/.

17 Note: The full story of the move of the chapel originally appeared in Collegeville Institute's *Bearings Online*, December 18, 2014, https://collegevilleinstitute.org/bearings/moving-church/.

18 Some parts of the chapter were originally published on the Episcopal Church Vital Practices blog.